to MY MOTHER

*who taught us that Christians
love one another*

PROGRESS AGAINST PREJUDICE

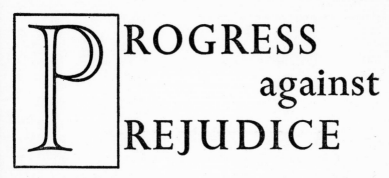

PROGRESS against PREJUDICE

THE CHURCH CONFRONTS THE RACE PROBLEM

By ROBERT ROOT

friendship press   NEW YORK

Library of Congress Catalog Card Number: 57–6158

COPYRIGHT, 1957, BY FRIENDSHIP PRESS, INC.
PRINTED IN THE UNITED STATES OF AMERICA

CONTENTS

Preface   ix

1 The Court, the Nation, and
   the Negro   3

2 The Churches Meet the Critics   18

3 The Challenge from Roman
   Catholicism   36

4 Can the Races Be Integrated
   in the Church?   49

5 Integration: No Longer an
   Experiment   65

6 How High Does Equality Go?   90

7 Of Roots and Branches   106

8 A Typical City—Case Study   124

9 Bureaus and Brotherhood   147

ACKNOWLEDGMENTS

I WANT to thank several who have helped me collect material for this book, especially my colleague, Roland E. Wolseley, and Edwin H. Maynard, Methodist editor. Appreciation also goes to other editors of the Protestant press, notably Herman C. Ahrens Jr., Theodore C. Braun, George Walker Buckner Jr., and William E. Leidt; to Erik W. Modean, Ralph Stoody, and Wendell Kellogg, pioneers of church public relations; to the Baptists' Bernice Cofer; and not least, to my patient editors at Friendship Press, William C. Walzer and Robert A. Elfers. Others unknown to me have also submitted material, read the manuscript, or made helpful suggestions. To all, no blame for any shortcomings, but warm appreciation for aid.

R. R.

PREFACE

I HAVE written this book in the hope that it will improve the relations between the races, especially in the church. But I do not write with a pretense of neutrality; my premise is that, like war, adultery, and greed, racism is sinful. I also start with the assumption that whites are the chief offenders, and I speak as one white man to another. I hope and believe that colored people will be interested in what the book has to say, but it would be futile if not dishonest for me to try to address disembodied, colorless spirits.

This is a mission book, but in a special sense. Mission boards have provided some fine leadership in interracial work, and again and again through the book appear the results of good mission thinking. Missions have been the leaven for much that is reported here. Some projects sponsored by missions are described as such. Only in part, however, is this book about missions as institutions—but it is *all* about the mission of each individual Christian. The very life of the downtown church often depends on more church members recognizing their duties to minority groups. And as Negroes get better housing, more and more of us who are white will have to face up to "missionary responsibilities" in our neighborhoods. In a larger sense, therefore, this is a mission book, for its purpose is to "evangelize" the ordinary church member by informing him about how the churches are advancing—and lagging—in the race field.

Language is a problem in a book like this. At best, writers about race are plagued with words like "antisegregation" and "integrationist." Arguments can be started at the drop of a hat about the respective uses of "ethnic" and "race," "inclusive" and "interracial," and so on; gobbledeygookists talk sometimes as if curing our semantics would cure our bigotry, but it won't! I have tried to avoid the legalistic and scientistic and have chosen where I could the simple, well-known word, with clarity as a major goal. After this sentence, I shall even drop quotation marks in referring to the "white" churches, because everyone knows what they are—though we can agree with the purist that they should be simply "Christian"!

I have striven for a rough sort of balance among denominations, but have tried to use the most interesting material I could get, regardless of source. I have not attempted at each step to include all possible illustrations. A much longer book would be needed to be really comprehensive.

In short, the important thing about the text that follows is not the semantics nor the credit, but the inspiration of the many who have acted like real Christians; I hope that their example will be clear and compelling.

Syracuse, New York   ROBERT ROOT
November 1, 1956

PROGRESS AGAINST PREJUDICE

I THE COURT, THE NATION, AND THE NEGRO

I
N CENTRAL NEBRASKA, WHERE THE Dismal River flows into the Middle Loup River, is Dunning, a small community that rarely gets into the headlines outside the sandhill cattle area. But in the fall of 1955 the town was on the press wires because its top school official had tried out an idea.

Superintendent C. Floyd Boydston had been having trouble getting teachers. Specifically, he could not find an instructor in bookkeeping, typewriting, and English. Since none seemed available in the vicinity, where could he find one? Pondering that question, he got his idea.

"I purposely turned to the South and looked for a Negro," he explained later.

In a bakery at Magnolia, Mississippi, Boydston found the man he wanted. Charles Carpenter, a twenty-three-year-old Negro teacher, one of thirteen children of a sharecropper, had been graduated with honors from Xavier University in New Orleans. Now he was working while he looked for a school job. Would he come to Dunning?

"I didn't hesitate one second," Teacher Carpenter said. "I was hitchhiking to Nebraska the day after I was told I was hired."

In Dunning, for reasons they couldn't define, some individuals were lukewarm. But their mild opposition vanished when the new instructor arrived. He was met with a warm handshake everywhere.

"I knew my big step was a good one," Mr. Carpenter recalled later.

The new teacher's students have kept him busy learning to ride horses and hunt and fish, and he and a white coach "batch" together in a rented house.

After the Associated Press carried the news, the superintendent got eleven letters. Five condemned him, six commended. Half of the praising letters were from the South.

One factor influencing his decision to ignore the color line, said Mr. Boydston, was the fact that he is a church member.

Did the church give him the idea?

"I can't say that my religion gave me the idea of hiring a Negro teacher," he replied, "but it certainly supported the action after we located a Negro who was qualified and interested."

He added significantly, "I am not aware that Christianity, as explained in the Bible, ever placed the races in varying esteem of God."

¶The Court Lights a Fuse

The Dunning story speaks to two of the nation's major race problems. One is the question of school segregation. The other concerns the opportunities that Negroes have to get good jobs. Significantly, what happened in Dunning also underlines the part the Christian can play when he simply puts his convictions to work.

School integration got its biggest push, of course, from the 1954 Supreme Court decision against segregation in public schools. Within the next year, five hundred schools were integrated.

In spite of widely publicized cases of friction, the National Association for the Advancement of Colored People (NAACP) says: "There have been scores of unheralded instances of Negro children being welcomed by their new white schoolmates and teachers. Indeed, this has been the rule."

In general, integration is advancing fastest where the proportion of Negroes is smallest. The real progress in the last two or three years has been in a row of border states. Going across a map from the West, we can list Arizona, New Mexico, Oklahoma, Kansas, Missouri, West Virginia, Maryland, and Delaware in this group. The three largest cities that have integrated are in this band—St. Louis, Washington, and Baltimore.

Between these states and the really Deep South are Texas, Arkansas, Tennessee, and Kentucky, where some integration is beginning. In these four states, it is safe to predict, some of the big news of future advances will come. For example,

in 1955 after the first flush of compliance with the court decision had ended, Corpus Christi, in southern Texas, approved desegregation. At the same time, federally-controlled
Oak Ridge, Tennessee, opened its schools to one hundred
Negro children. In the fall of 1956, troops had to maintain
order as Negroes began to attend schools in Sturgis, Kentucky, and Clinton, Tennessee, and the Kentucky town
segregated again shortly after the troops left. But meantime,
Louisville, Kentucky, became the largest Southern city to
integrate the schools, and there was no serious incident.

The strongest opposition to the court has come in the
crescent of southeastern states—Louisiana, Mississippi, Alabama, Florida, Georgia, South Carolina, North Carolina,
and Virginia. These are states where a majority of the
citizens in some sections are Negroes. However, the same
is true in parts of Texas, Arkansas, and Tennessee.

But even in this Deep South the front against integration is not solid. Wake County, North Carolina, for example,
voted to end segregation in September, 1956. Some districts
in Alexandria, Virginia, have also been desegregated.

Here, too, have been the casualties. In Lake County,
Florida, the school board fired Don Conway, a math
teacher; he had supported a student petition urging that
the high school keep some children whom the sheriff had
decided were Negroes.

Mr. Conway said, "If giving the kids my moral support
in what I consider a Christian act is guilt, then I'm guilty."

Segregation had been rolled back far enough for a survey
in twenty-four communities, made before the court decision,
to conclude that the effort had been generally successful in

the area studied. The authors of this report, *Schools in Transition*, financed by the Ford Foundation, found that the change came most easily where there had been other community experiences in interracial cooperation. This conclusion is borne out by the success in desegregating the Baltimore schools. There Superintendent John H. Fisher pointed out that color bars had previously gone down in the theaters and in police and fire departments.

The Ford survey also showed that the problems were not with the children but with the parents. As a Missouri school paper put it: "We high school students will take the change in stride if the adults don't make a big production of it."

In city after city, integration came pleasantly. Take Topeka, Kansas, for example. This community was one of the losing defendants in a famous court case, but it had been an unenthusiastic litigant. Months before the court acted, Topeka had decided to merge the elementary schools.

"The kids took to each other," one principal told an Associated Press reporter. "The parents cooperated splendidly. As to the teachers—well, one teacher accidentally wasn't assigned any Negro pupils in her class. She came to me asking for a rearrangement. She was afraid people might think her attitude was responsible."

In Oklahoma City, transition has also started. In its Lincoln School, there are Negroes, Indians, Mexicans, Filipinos, and Japanese, as well as Caucasian children. The PTA took an early stand that Negro mothers should be invited to its meetings, and one of them was soon named hospitality committee chairman.

One of the PTA mothers said, commenting on integration, "It goes along with what we try to teach our children in church, at home, and in school—we are all God's children."

A little different religious idea got into the nation's news when the Rev. William Thomas (Bill) Carter, a chunky, gray-haired preacher of forty-nine in Hobbs, New Mexico, argued that "God segregated the three children of Noah."

A Texan, Mr. Carter was a field laborer for twenty years and served a term on a Texas chain gang, according to *The New York Times*. But he was "saved" in 1937 and was named a lay preacher by the Southeastern Baptist Association. In the face of opposition from the New Mexico Baptist Convention, he organized a group against desegregation in this oil town. But his efforts failed. White children started going to school harmoniously with the Negro children of Hobbs.

Elsewhere, some whites were so strong for integration that they tried to break the separation down for their own children in places where the court decision had not yet been accepted.

In Louisville, Kentucky, eleven-year-old David Rogers Russell became the first white child to enroll in an all-Negro school. He and his mother were visiting for a few months with Mrs. Abbie Jackson, who belonged to the United Church Women (of which Mrs. Russell had also been a member). David had attended school with children of twenty-eight nationalities in Tokyo, Japan, where his father, the Rev. Galen Russell, was pastor of the Tokyo Union Church. David's mother earnestly requested that he now be permitted to go to the Negro school, and she was "exceedingly happy and very proud" when he was given the right.

With less success, Robert W. Rempfer, a white college teacher of mathematics, and his wife tried to get their son and daughter into Negro schools. Stymied, Professor Rempfer, an instructor at predominantly Negro Fisk University, took the issue to Federal court, where it was still pending in the fall of 1956.

Meantime, Judy Genier, of Moriah Center, New York, got interested in Allen High School, a Negro school in North Carolina, when she heard the white principal give a talk about it at a Methodist meeting near her home.

"I just feel as if I've wasted my life," Judy told her mother afterward. She decided she would like to let the Negro girls "know what it is like to have a white sister," and she got permission to attend the school, which is operated by the Methodist Church. At thirteen, Judy became the only white student among 130 Negroes. From the White House, Mrs. Dwight D. Eisenhower wrote to praise her for "making the road to integration a shorter one."

At the college level, integration has been coming for a longer time. Many colleges, North and South, were admitting Negro undergraduates even before 1954, and several Southern college editors took a friendly view of the court's decision. "If we are wise," said the *Daily Tar Heel* of the University of North Carolina, "we will welcome Negro North Carolinians to our schools and to our universities." In the fall of 1955, the first three Negro students in its 166-year history were admitted as undergraduates at that university. Texas and Tennessee also moved toward integration. With two thousand Negroes already in mixed Southern colleges, the impression grew that segregation in higher education is doomed.

¶What Are the Job Prospects?

Some people object to the end of school segregation with the claim that it will mean unemployment for Negro teachers. That danger is real, but as the story of Dunning, Nebraska, suggests, steps toward equality also bring job opportunities. In such communities as Kansas City, where segregation has been ended, large numbers of Negro instructors are still employed. During the first eight years that segregation was banned in New Jersey, the number of Negro teachers rose from 479 to 645. Unsegregated Connecticut has 130 Negro teachers in public schools of thirty towns, and New York City is seeking Southern Negro teachers.

Fair employment laws have brought improvement in job opportunities for the colored worker, and the experience of working side by side has cut white hostility. Equality is still far away, however. Any Northerner who inquires about his own community will doubtless find that Negroes do not often get jobs above the janitorial or semiskilled level. In the South, according to reports of both the Urban League and the National Planning Association, there has been some improvement. Though the Negro's wages typically still lag far behind white salaries, in New Orleans some Negroes have moved into "higher level, traditionally white" jobs at the same pay as white workers.

Some labor unions have helped bring change by insisting

that Negroes should have equal rights to membership and jobs. The United Auto Workers forced local members back on the job in Memphis when they quit because a Negro was made a welder. The leaders also expelled a Texas union for excluding Mexicans.

The UAW, incidentally, has published a twelve-page pamphlet of special interest to church people. On the cover is a drawing of whites and Negroes going into a church, with the title, *Souls Don't Have Color*. The booklet argues against prejudice among Christians. "Where churches do practice discrimination," says Walter Reuther in a foreword, "it is widely accepted in communities. . . . Where churches practice discrimination, many employers pit white workers against Negro workers to hold down wages and working conditions. Churches are the conscience of communities."

Following a Washington conference in the fall of 1955, Vice-President Richard M. Nixon, as the chairman, announced its main finding: The big problem of discrimination in industry is not so much in hiring as in equality of opportunity afterwards. Industrialists at the meeting reported that fears about integration had proved unjustified. Gwilym A. Price, head of Westinghouse Electric, said there are "hard-headed business" reasons for hiring Negro workers. His company has some Negro supervisors over white and mixed departments.

Helping set the pattern of nondiscrimination in employment was the Federal Government's actions against segregation in the armed forces.

Federal action, following up the school decision, also began to end the separation of the races in recreation and transportation. It was the Supreme Court again which ruled in November, 1955, that segregation in public parks, playgrounds, and golf courses is illegal. Before the month was out, the Interstate Commerce Commission also decreed that racial segregation on trains and buses that cross state lines must end. One of the biggest resulting problems was with "white" and "colored" waiting rooms. How could interstate and intrastate travelers be unscrambled in a station? Seeing the impossibilities, many Southern cities quietly desegregated their waiting rooms.

¶The Negro Looks for a House

Housing was another problem to which the school decision drew attention, for mixing in schools is limited as long as the races are segregated in living areas. But here the Federal Government was slower to move. Interracial leaders protested that federally-supported programs still were putting up lily-white housing and even evicting Negroes from areas where they had lived.

"The housing program of the Government continued to be the greatest single force in the nation promoting residential segregation," complained the NAACP.

Some critics suggested that the President issue an executive order denying mortgage guarantees to any builder barring Negroes. Nevertheless, one quarter of all Negroes in public housing live next door or across the hall from white neighbors.

One of the striking things about housing integration is that many do not realize it is already far advanced. A study by the Philadelphia Housing Association showed that 88 per cent of all Negro families and 22 per cent of all white families in Philadelphia live in blocks in which there is some racial integration. In over a fourth of the city's blocks, Negro and white families live side by side.

The University of California found that all-white neighborhoods in San Francisco were accepting Negroes and Chinese-Americans without fuss or bother.

"They tend to be treated in the same anonymous or impersonal way as any other newcomers in a big city neighborhood," summarized Professor Davis McEntire. One quarter of the people interviewed did not even know that minority group members were living near them!

From different sections of the country come many other indications that segregation in housing is crumbling.

In Waverly, Iowa, a Negro Air Force officer hesitated to move into an apartment because of racial pressure, but town residents held a meeting to present him with keys to an apartment and a petition urging him to accept. He did.

In Portland, Oregon, a sixteen-unit cooperative project was opened with six white and ten nonwhite families.

At Stockton, California, Mexican-Americans, Negroes, Filipinos, and Orientals live among whites in an interracial development started in 1951.

Negroes from a nearby ghetto began to come into a two-hundred-home project at San Antonio, Texas. Many whites moved out. In such cases, some want to leave the Negroes; others like to sell for the boosted prices Negroes have to pay for houses (in San Antonio, $200 to $600 higher, at one time). But some whites, saying that they never had better neighbors, are staying. Significantly, a person driving down the street can't tell which homes are "Negro" and which "white," says *House and Home* magazine.

At Taylor, Texas, which got into the news awhile back by naming a Negro "Man of the Year," an interracial project has operated quietly since 1952. Its seventy units include thirty-five Negro families and thirty-three white and Latin American families. This project was begun to clear a slum area in which there were serious outbreaks of polio. One result was that cases of polio and other diseases dropped in the section.

In New York City, a community center headed by the vice-president of the Bronx Real Estate Board began a program to "break up ghetto living." The group is encouraging interracial tenancy in three large-scale housing projects. Its goal is eventual desegregation of such areas as Harlem. In encouragement, the chairman of the city Housing Authority said, "There's not a single public housing project in Greater New York in which Negroes and whites are not living side by side in harmony."

¶*Showcase and Symbol*

Progress in race relations has, at best, been uneven.

White Citizens' Councils have been organized in some states to put the economic screws on those who befriend Negroes. Many Americans who felt that lynching had ended were shocked when fourteen-year-old Negro Emmett Till was killed in Mississippi, and United States prestige plummeted as dozens of European papers headlined this "whistle murder case" as "scandalous" and "monstrous."

On the other hand, Negroes have made a lot of progress in

entertainment and sports. Marian Anderson, the famous singer, has had her debut at the Metropolitan Opera. A Negro has played baseball with whites in Memphis, and a Negro student participated in the Sugar Bowl game after Georgia Tech students assailed their segregationist governor for being behind the times.

The Harris County Medical Society in Texas has opened the door to Negro doctors. A Cleveland newspaper named a Negro to head its seven-man staff of police reporters, and the Nashville *Tennessean* ran on its front page the story and picture of a Negro Episcopal family. For the first time, Negroes have recently been named to such posts as Federal parole board chief, vice-mayor of Cincinnati, and justice of the New York State Supreme Court. And in the Protestant churches—but that is getting ahead of the story. . . .

Perhaps the whole confusing picture can best be brought into focus with a look at a single city in transition, Washington, D.C., a symbol of the whole nation's struggle with the problem.

The Negro population in the capital has been increasing and now is more than half the total. Washingtonians are citizens without a vote; law provides that Congress must be the capital's city council. In 1953 the Supreme Court held an old Washington antidiscrimination law to be valid, and the commissioners of the District of Columbia announced that they would enforce it in eating places. Literally overnight, restaurants opened to all races.

Negroes now may not only dine in any restaurant in town, but they may stay in any hotel, attend any movie house, swim in any public pool, or play golf on any public course.

Symbolic of the shift is the treatment of Marian Anderson. In 1939 she was refused the use of Constitution Hall, so she sang on the steps of the Lincoln Memorial; since then she has given three concerts in the hall.

The change was so marked that the American Friends Service Committee, Quaker-led agency, decided to close out a four-year project to overcome segregation in the District.

"These years, 1951 to 1955, proved to be the most dramatic for the history of the city and for the story of desegregation," says the AFSC report. "In these years, the city made changes in its racial practices so rapidly as to be startling to even the most optimistic."

The report added, however, that much remains to be done in medical service, housing, employment, and *religious bodies.*

When the organization began its work, there were some nonsegregated areas of life. Buses carried passengers without segregation, and Negro employees of the government worked side by side with white. Then "art" cinemas began to admit patrons without discrimination, and some restaurants opened up even before 1953. A few hotels eased restrictions, though the policies of some are still shifting and confused. In 1954, for the first time at a downtown hotel, a group of Negro school girls in white gowns and elbow-length white gloves made a fashionable debut.

Here are some other notable Washington advances of recent years:

The district medical association admits some Negroes.

Cuban Negroes play on the American League baseball team.

The transit system hires Negro operators.

Nineteen of twenty-four public housing projects are open to all.

One of the big tests of segregation in Washington came when the Supreme Court ordered integration in the schools. In 1952, Presidential Candidate Eisenhower had declared, "Segregation in the nation's capital must be abolished." The day after the court decision, the President told the commissioners that he wanted Washington to lead the way, to be the showcase.

The school system began the change slowly—so slowly that some Negro leaders protested. Hundreds of white students struck against desegregation in nine schools. But the opposition fizzled. By the fall of 1955, beginning their second year with desegregation, the Washington schools were quiet and happy. Superintendent of Schools Hobart M. Corning said, "I have quite a number of letters on file from parents who say that, originally, they were unhappy at the prospect of having a Negro teacher for their children, but now they are singing the praises of those teachers."

It was such progress that led the Friends committee to its conclusion.

"For the individual Negro, there is freedom of movement and greater opportunity; for the Negro community, there is a lowering of barriers, the beginning of a merger with the whole; for the city, and the nation it symbolizes, there is greater dignity."

Eugene Davis, president of the Washington chapter of the NAACP, put it all in a capsule: "Things in general are going beautifully."

2 THE CHURCHES MEET
THE CRITICS

MANY COMPLACENT PROTESTANTS were shaken up a bit when *Time* magazine declared awhile back that "11 A.M. Sunday is the most segregated hour of the week." But no one denied the essential truth of the observation. The Christian church remains one of America's most segregated institutions, while integration makes the broad advances noted in the first chapter.

The *Time* comment underlined a fact that is becoming more and more obvious to sensitive Christians: *The world outside the American church is becoming increasingly critical of racial discrimination among those who say they follow Christ.*

Writers and speakers are forever putting

Christians on the spot for acting like Pharisees. For example, the Providence (R.I.) *Journal* printed a series by James N. Rhea, "Jim Crow Goes to Church." Dr. Barnett R. Bricker, a leading rabbi, urging a joint religious attack on segregation, stated confidently that Jews would uphold church members if they made "a genuine move to give reality to their beliefs in men's brotherhood."

Dr. Dagobert D. Runes, in *Letters to My Daughter,* penned acidly: "I wonder if those church people think that when Christ called the children to him they came in two groups—the white ones separately and the black ones separately. If they would only hesitate to think what a blasphemous farce they make of Christianity. . . ." [1]

And in a sociology book, *Minorities and the American Promise,* not aimed for church readers at all, Stewart G. and Mildred W. Cole wrote (italics mine):

The rank and file of church people who are also Americans have yet to discover *the real outreach of their responsibility to minority peoples.* Their obligation *cannot be discharged by the adoption of well-considered resolutions,* by the exhortation of the clergy, or even by the sponsorship of formal interracial programs, however useful these practices may be. . . . When these people begin to *square their precepts and practices,* Christianity will affirm its moral integrity in the intercultural field; how white Anglo-Protestants and Catholics choose to meet this challenge *will determine* in no small measure the social dynamics of organized religion *for years to come.*[2]

One of the strongest criticisms of church practice comes from the NAACP. In a booklet, *Target for 1963,* this organi-

---

[1] New York, Philosophical Library, 1954. Used by permission.
[2] Published by Harper and Brothers, New York, 1954. Used by permission.

zation says that "a few churches" have lowered color bars
and that while segregated churches cannot be brought to
court "for their rejection of the Christian doctrine of universal brotherhood," they can be challenged. Then it states:

Repeatedly the church has expressed contrition because of its
failure to meet the issue of race in accordance with Christian doctrine. This failure is often deplored at church conventions, but
little has been done in the individual churches to rectify the all
but universal separation of the races in worship.

The NAACP, through its church division and its branches, will
continue to confront the churches with this moral contradiction
and to urge the practice as well as the preaching of Christianity.

In 1944, Gunnar Myrdal, a Swedish sociologist, in *An
American Dilemma* wrote a most intensive study of American
Negro life:

The average Southern white man, for natural reasons, can only
be grateful not to have his stand on race relations exposed to the
teachings of Christianity. . . . The moral situation is not alto-
gether different in the North. . . . It is . . . true that many
white churches in the North have a few Negro members, and that
they rarely would turn away Negro visitors who came to a service.
But usually they cannot afford to let the Negro membership grow
too large. . . . The great majority of white churches, in the
North as well as in the South, thus do not want to have a substantial Negro membership. The great majority of Negroes do not
seem to want to join white churches, even if they are allowed. As
usual the caste separation has been fortified by its own effects.[1]

Alan Paton, author of *Cry, the Beloved Country,* who attended the assembly of the World Council of Churches at
Evanston in 1954, also looked into the race problem and

---

[1] Published by Harper and Brothers, New York, 1944. Used by permission.

wrote his findings up in *Collier's*. Do we come off any better with the novelist than the sociologist?

Perhaps a little better. Paton listed the churches among the American groups that have been effectively fighting segregation. But there was a prophetic ring as he wrote about one Negro family trying to live in a Chicago section where they were hated:

The Howards lived behind boarded windows, their children in terror, all youngness gone, in a cacophony of bombs and curses and smashing glass. Christians did this, not knowing or not caring for the fierce words of their Lord.

So both the secular world and our foreign visitors rip at our hypocritical masks. It is no surprise that the Communists also are scathing about our failures. But the criticism abroad is much more widespread than the Communists alone can foment.

This point was made in an article in the American church press by Roland E. Wolseley, author of *Face to Face with India*. He pointed out that Americans in Asia are prodded by such questions as, "You Americans talk a lot about democracy, but when are you going to treat the Negro people of your country democratically?"

What can you say to such questions? You can reply, of course, that our problem is like India's caste problem. But as Professor Wolseley pointed out, that only explains; it does not justify an American caste system. He added significantly: "Indian Christians who asked about race in America were more difficult to answer than were Hindus or Moslems, because Indian Christians expect so much more in the way of Christian behavior."

The Supreme Court ruling against school segregation reminded us all how much the eyes of the whole world, and
not only of India, were upon our handling of the race question.

In England, the frequently anti-American London *Daily
Mirror* said the decision would rank with the Emancipation
Proclamation. A *Daily Mail* columnist wrote: "The ruling
has helped to spike the Communist propaganda that Americans treat their colored people like dogs and worse." French
papers called it "a victory of justice over race prejudice."

Even *Die Burger* in Capetown, provincial capital of segregated South Africa, gave praise of a sort when it worried:
"The most important bastion in America's color bar policy
has now fallen."

In South Africa as well as India, however, students rose
and stood at silent attention when this court decision was
announced. Recalling that fact, foreign students at the 1955
Quadrennial of the Student Volunteer Movement in Athens,
Ohio, agreed that the ruling was the strongest blow the
United States had struck against communism. At that conference, which gathered many young missionaries-to-be, foreign Christian leaders declared that a primary task of the
church is to smash racial barriers everywhere.

That was a familiar emphasis for old-time missionaries,
who have long contended that racial snobbery undercuts
their work. The president of the Southern Baptist Convention has warned that defiance of the Supreme Court "will
endanger our foreign mission work throughout thirty-five
areas of the earth and play right into the hands of the
Communists." The Division of Foreign Missions of the Na-

tional Council of Churches declared: "Every act of un-brotherliness and injustice by citizens of our country speaks more loudly abroad than do the sermons of missionaries and pastors abroad about reconciliation."

Just how loudly it speaks was indicated when an Indian clergyman, the Rev. M. A. Thomas, bitterly described his reaction to attendance at a segregated service in Georgia: "When I discovered that the church doors were closed to Negroes, it was impossible for me to worship. When the choir sang the words 'My Lord and Saviour,' I asked myself, 'Whose Lord and Saviour?'"

If American Christians needed proof that men and women around the world were looking to see what they did about race, this was the answer to their doubts.

¶An Optimist vs. a Pessimist

The court decision to end school segregation made many churchmen face up to discrimination squarely for the first time. The secular world, already scornful of Christian failures to practice Christian brotherhood, now seemed bent on forcing Christians to be brotherly whether they wanted to be or not. Have the churches reacted favorably to this pressure?

"I think we can be very much heartened by the churches' reactions to the decision," says Mr. Optimist. "Church bodies and individual Christians all over the country have come out in the open and strongly urged the end of segregation."

"Yes," replies Mr. Pessimist, "but our leaders aren't leading us fast enough. I agree with Herman Long, a Congregationalist official. He says one of our big problems today is 'a vacillating religious leadership that robs the community of a voice of conscience and gives no moral support for the Supreme Court order.'"

"That's too hard on the preachers. Hodding Carter, a newspaper publisher in Greenville, Mississippi, says: 'I am sure that the support given the court (by churchmen) helped to ease tensions on both sides of the Mason-Dixon and color lines.' And: 'If we would pay more attention to what preachers say and less to what the politicians say about banning segregation in the public schools, we would be better off.'"

"If a minister listened to Carter, however, he'd probably lose his job."

"No, he'd have the whole church behind him. It happened that the board of the National Council of Churches was meeting in Chicago when the court gave its decision. Do you know what the board members did? They got out a resolution right away saying that it 'gives a clear status in law to a fundamental Christian and American principle.' They didn't hedge. They urged 'the churches and individual Christians . . . to exert their influence and leadership' to implement it."

"Resolutions are easy to pass, but they don't represent what the people in the pews really think. Let me give you an example. Here's an article in the *Alabama Christian Advocate*. It's by Owen Love, an Alabama school principal and Methodist Sunday school teacher. He says Negro teachers understand Negro pupils better, and he asks: 'Do we not want to recognize that to put Negro children in competition with white children will fasten upon them a real inferiority complex?' "

"That won't wash. You can't find a reputable scientist who will say one race is naturally superior to another. You take some of these bright Negro kids—maybe it's the white kids who will get the inferiority complex!"

"You don't have to lecture me! I know that. I'm just explaining what people think. Some people would say the inferiority was due to environment. This writer has a lot to say about history. He says the Fourteenth Amendment is based on Northern guns during the War Between the States, and——"

"Speaking of history," Mr. Optimist breaks in, "James McBride Dabbs says in *The Christian Century* that segregationists tend to be blind to the realities of both past and present. He's an active Southern Presbyterian elder—lives near Mayesville, South Carolina. So it's all the more important when he points out that the White Citizens' Councils, which have been springing up to fight for segregation, have been forcing 'men of sensitive conscience,' especially preachers, into openly backing desegregation."

"O.K. But did you see the hullaballoo that Dabbs's article stirred up? Here's a letter in the *Century* from Fred H. Ford, stated clerk of the Presbytery of New Orleans. He says race prejudice is just a mistaken name for 'racial antipathy, inherent in nature.' Next to it is a letter from a Mississippi fellow who says the Negro is naturally different: 'You can't change human nature by education, Christianity, religion, or anything else.' Those men will never favor desegregation."

"They're a minority."

"Are they? Did you know that a prosegregation petition was circulated in North Carolina that deplores all efforts to identify 'integration of the races with Christianity'? It says Bible study shows that Christ 'never said one word about the race problem.'"

"Here's a fellow who doesn't agree. Ben L. Smith, superintendent of schools at Greensboro, North Carolina, was one of the first officials in the South to line up behind the Supreme Court decision. He challenged the Methodists at the state conference to stand up with the schools, and declared: 'As Christians, we must set an example for others to follow.'"

Mr. Pessimist shrugs, as if to say there are exceptions to all rules, and goes on with the debate:

"Church bigwigs don't represent the rank and file. The Rev. George S. Reamey, editor of the *Virginia Methodist Advocate,* says: 'Virtually all of the church groups have come out in favor of nonsegregation in the churches. But as so often happens, church leaders do not always represent the real feelings of their constituents.'"

"Do you know what happened in South Carolina when one Methodist church tried to line up church support *for* segregation? Only three out of 771 churches responded to the appeal."

"I cite to you, too, the *Baptist Standard* of Dallas, Texas, which says the court ruling should be accepted but suggests voluntary separation. 'We believe that the vast majority of Negroes, especially in the South, prefer separate schools just as they prefer separate churches,' the editor writes."

"But J. Claude Evans, editor of the *South Carolina Meth-*

odist Advocate, has come out against segregation. He says desegregation is inevitable."

"O.K., but in the *North Carolina Christian Advocate* Ralph I. Epps says: 'I have not been convinced by any means that nonsegregation is God's will for North Carolina Methodism. A Methodism free from racial segregation could be full of something far worse. It is still my conviction that a Christian brotherhood can be achieved within the bounds of segregation. Racial discrimination, as such, has no part whatsoever in God's will.' "

"Well, in the South you're apt to run into———"

"It's not only the South. I know that old argument that Northerners use to wiggle out of responsibility. Sure, blame the South. But Northern Christians favor segregation, too. Here's a letter in the *Lutheran Standard*, signed by the initials of someone in Ohio. This writer figures that Isaiah 13:14, about everyone fleeing into his own land, somehow supports discrimination. He says, 'It looks to me like God wants us to stay among our own people.' "

"I've got a Southerner who uses stronger language than that—and on the other side. He is Julian S. Orrell, a twenty-nine-year-old minister at Ivor, Virginia, who has lived most of his life in that state. He wrote the Southern Baptist *Religious Herald* that the desegregation ruling is 'in accord with the teachings, life, mind, and example of Christ as interpreted by reputable Bible scholarship for hundreds of years.' "

"Yes, but—"

"And in the *Christian Advocate*, Mason Crum, professor of religion at Duke University, says he's not disturbed by

the decision, nor are most Southerners. 'You may talk to
farmers, laborers, trainmen, and professional people, and
they will generally agree that the decision was inevitable
and right.' "

"But—"

"Just a minute. Do you remember how the board of
education in Georgia barred any teacher favoring mixed
classes? Well, that riled the Protestant Episcopal Bishop of
North Georgia. He said that this effort at state control of
thought 'lines us up with Nazi Germany or Communist
Russia.' "

"But—"

"Hold on. I've still got a statement made by the women
church leaders of fifteen Southern states. Fifteen—get that.
It's important. These representatives of the United Church
Women said the school decision gave an 'opportunity of
translating into reality Christian and democratic ideals.'
They felt 'impelled to promote a Christian society in which
segregation is no longer a burden upon the human spirit.' "

"Women are apt to take a less realistic view. Now the
men—"

"All right, if you want men: Methodist Bishop William T.
Watkins in Memphis warned that 'the church that says it's a
follower of Jesus Christ must not allow the state to get ahead
of it in this march for Christianity.' Across the Mississippi,
the Metropolitan Church Federation of St. Louis praised
the court decision and asked its 550 member churches to
abolish their own segregation. The Kentucky Methodist
conference also asked members 'to seek to have the mind of
Christ' in the coming social adjustment."

"That doesn't necessarily mean they favored the adjustment."

"Take it as you like. But then look at a town that became world famous because eleven Negro children started to attend an all-white school—Milford, Delaware. *Presbyterian Life* sent four reporters there and found 'an almost palpable air of fear.' That so-called 'National Association for the Advancement of White People' (NAAWP) was telephoning white parents and threatening to harm their kids if they went to school. I suppose you figure that the ministers ran for cover."

"Look—no one wants to stick his neck out. I remember the paper—"

"Well, you're wrong. There are eleven clergymen in Milford, including the Roman Catholic priest. Nine of them agreed to be interviewed, and all of those with school-age children were sending their children to school in spite of the threats."

"That means there were still two who weren't sticking their necks out, just as I said—"

"One of those two was a Negro minister who was afraid of saying anything that would hurt his people. The other was, I admit, a white minister who was keeping his children from school. But the thing that impresses me is that those favoring segregation warned one Protestant minister that his worship services would be boycotted unless he soft-pedaled his race views—but he didn't, and the people kept coming."

"But one of the leaders of the NAAWP was the Rev. Manaen Warrington, who has a lot to say about how God upholds segregation. I grant you, the Methodists defrocked him, but it shows you the kind of religious leader who can get a hearing. He thinks that the Bible is referring to whites, not the Jewish nation, as 'the Chosen People!' "

"A man like that is to be pitied. He's not typical. The prosegregation people in Milford felt the churches had said *too much* for integration. But the old views are shifting. 'No bigoted mind will be changed by denominational declarations,' one Milford minister said, 'but the spirit of Christ does change bigoted minds, and it's happened in every church in Milford.' "

"I agree that resolutions don't do much good."

"They can stiffen backbones that are weakening. The presbytery of which Milford is a part adopted a resolution calling on Presbyterians to refrain from any school boycott. The Maryland-Delaware Council of Churches supported the court decision as 'Christian and American.' While the Milford disturbance was at its height, the clergy of Sussex County, Delaware, declared: 'If God is not the God of the Negro, neither is he the God of the white. If he is not the God of all, he is not the God of any.' That puts it pretty straight. Moreover, two Methodist conferences of the area adopted integration resolutions. Such resolutions change the climate of opinion."

"I'm a lot more interested in action than resolutions."

"All right. Then you'd be interested in the fact that 97 per cent of the mothers in the Milford Presbyterian Women's Association kept their children in school. 'Thanks mostly to the strong Biblical preaching Mr. Kepler has been giving us all along, we knew what God wanted us to do,' one mother said of their preacher. 'In our association we defi-

nitely place integration . . . on what the Bible teaches us
about the love of Christ for all men.'

"Then there was the Milford layman who was ruffled by
the calls urging parents to keep their children out of school
and got on the phone to call friends and tell them why they
should keep the children in school.

"And there was another layman who was asked whether
it was true he was a 'nigger-lover.' He gave a classic reply:
'Why, yes, I am. I try to follow Christ in my life, and the
way my Bible reads, he loved all men and died for them.
So he must be a Negro-lover, and what's good enough for
him is certainly good enough for me.' " [1]

"That's a good comeback. But I notice these examples
you're giving are from what I'd call border states. You'll run
into some tolerance there. But take the Southern Baptists—"

"What about the Southern Baptists? Their record looks
pretty good. The *Alabama Baptist* urged 'all our people to
be prayerful, sane, and Christian in facing this new situation.' In Georgia *The Christian Index* declared propheti-
cally: 'If we rise to the challenge, the future will look back
into our present as one of Christianity's finest years.' In their
1954 convention, the Southern Baptists declared the court
ruling was in harmony 'with the Christian principles of
equal justice and love of all men.' "

"Look, let's be realistic. Everybody knows that in the
really Deep—"

"The realistic thing is to see what Southerners say. The
Executive Committee of the Georgia Council of Churches
urged Christians to oppose 'every racial discrimination.'

[1] Adapted by permission from *Presbyterian Life.*

When their attorney general said he would not represent Georgia at court hearings on bringing desegregation, three church bodies urged him to go. *We're being realistic, remember.* Well, in Virginia, the ministers of Warren County declared that segregation is contrary to the gospel; at Woodstock, the ministerial association urged an end to segregation; that association includes a Negro Methodist, by the way. In Mississippi, the Episcopal diocese got out a pamphlet saying that church members could 'learn to live within the court's decision.' "

"But the votes aren't all that way. The North Alabama Methodist Conference asserted in 1954 that separate public schools should be maintained."

"That's true. But the conference later adopted a resolution that called on people to obey the law. Speaking of Methodists, the North Carolina Conference asserted that the court decision 'is a true interpretation of our Christian faith.' "

"It's different in South Carolina. Presbyterians there voted to continue segregation at church institutions. The South Carolina Methodist Conference said that 'voluntary separation is not contrary to the spirit and teaching of the Christian faith' where both races want it. It added: 'It is apparent to us that an attempt to integrate the races in our public schools without regard to their relative numbers would work grave injustice to many innocent persons, and in the present instances we fear that the Negro would suffer most, as he has often when those far removed from his everyday problems have undertaken to speak in his name.' "

"All right—even I won't contend that every church member favors school integration. Obviously a lot of them don't. But I submit that in general the Protestant churches have met the challenge that the state has given them in the court decision. Perhaps the most significant reactions have come from church bodies of the South. The Presbyterian Church, U.S. (Southern) supported the decision. Seven Episcopal dioceses of the South have done that or taken steps to desegregate the churches themselves. The Cumberland Presbyterian Church not only approved the decision but prepared materials helping the churches to adjust to the new situation."

"There are a lot of exceptions, though—"

"Granted. Protestant churches allow a lot of difference of opinion. They are not dictatorial, monolithic organizations. But on balance, I think the actions of recent months show that the Protestant churches in both North and South have been throwing a lot of weight against segregation."

"We'd throw a lot more if we were really Christian."

¶Missions and the Sense of Direction

Protestant missions lead in church efforts to meet the critics and bring more Christian attitudes and actions on race. Missions provide the planning and strategy boards that work out patterns of church life that may last for generations. They give the sense of direction.

"The mission job comes in the form of a thrust, where new ideas may sometimes be tried out in the churches or in programs the board controls," says one mission leader. "Or, as we are fond of saying, missions are the laboratory for testing steps toward social progress."

In any big city, especially where Negroes and perhaps Puerto Ricans are coming in, neighborhoods are changing. Churches must change or die. The mission job is to recommend how congregations should deal with the population shifts. Often mission money is needed to help the withering churches become self-supporting again with new congregations.

The change that came to all-white First Baptist Church in South Side Chicago during World War II is an example of mission leadership. Attendance was down to seventy-five. Then many Japanese-Americans, released from relocation centers, began to move into the neighborhood. It was suggested that new, separate churches be established, but the Chicago Baptist Missionary Society urged that First Baptist take them. It did. Soon there were numerous nisei in the congregation, and the Rev. Jitsuo Morikawa was named assistant minister and later, minister. When Negroes moved into the area, the church opened also to them. Today the active members are about 50 per cent Negro, 40 per cent white, and 10 per cent Oriental—because the planning and strategy of the mission group was accepted!

Similarly, the Presbyterians have a Chicago "mission church," Lawndale, supported by the presbytery missions. Here a Negro minister was brought in to serve the Negroes of the community, and some twenty old-line white members decided to stay and help make it an integrated church.

In the East Harlem Protestant Parish several men from Union Theological Seminary began work a few years ago among unchurched slum dwellers of New York. They got their start by borrowing $400 from the New York City

Mission Society to open store-front churches. These have been interracial from the start, and the idea has grown and spread to other cities.

In thirty states the Home Missions Division of the National Council not only provides religious services for migratory farm workers, with local church aid, but also tries to make the migrants' relations in the local communities friendly. Similarly the many community houses and youth work camps sponsored by missions establish healthy interracial patterns. Often church mission schools in this country contribute to better relations between the races. They train Negro young people to compete for good jobs and accustom them to interracial situations.

"The promotion of good will and understanding between Negro and white races is one way in which we are giving an area service," says a report of the Presbyterians' Gillespie-Selden Institute in Georgia. "The biracial staff in the School of Nursing is proving successful after a year's trial, and the biracial committees for the school and day care center have functioned without conflict. An integrated home nursing class of adults and young people will be repeated, as will be exchange programs with the white high school."

In such ways as these, missions plan advances and then consolidate them.

3 THE CHALLENGE FROM ROMAN CATHOLICISM

Nothing does more harm to the progress of Christianity and is more against its spirit than . . . race prejudice amongst Christians – Jacques Maritain, leading Roman Catholic philosopher.

 ROMAN CATHOLIC GIRL SAT DOWN and wrote to *Jubilee*, a picture magazine of her church, a letter which should be of wide interest to Protestants. Explaining that she was a secretary to a social agency of a Northern city, she said:

I'm the only Catholic in the place and was amazed at first that the colored children who come in know a Catholic if there's any outward indication—and expect from a Catholic an understanding and acceptance they don't even look for in persons of other religious backgrounds. . . . These children are receiving a great deal of love and understanding from all the staff—but they don't expect it from non-Catholics. And the non-Catholics are very curious to know why we have this reputation.

As far as I know, none of these colored children are Catholics themselves.

What frightens me and makes me sick at heart is the number of Catholics who will meet this expectation in a Negro acquaintance with a rebuff.[1]

Such a letter crisply reminds Protestants that what they do in race relations is always being measured against the Roman Catholic Christian standard. Roman Catholic action often challenges the rest of us to remember what Christians can do and should do.

¶The Archbishop Is Blind—to Color

One of the outstanding Roman Catholic leaders in the race area is the aging and almost blind Archbishop of New Orleans.

Joseph Francis Rummel was born in Baden, Germany, in 1876, the only child in a devout family. After the Rummels emigrated to New York, he attended a parochial school, became an altar boy, and decided to be a priest.

Rummel was ordained in Rome in 1902, became a clergyman in New York, then was named Bishop of Omaha. He has been prelate of the New Orleans archdiocese since 1935. There his interest in labor, politics, and race questions won him the unofficial title "Archbishop of Catholic Action."

Some years ago, the Archbishop's eyesight began to fail because of glaucoma. He had to start using a double magnifying glass to read small print, so a priest-secretary began

[1] Published in September, 1955. Used by permission.

to read aloud to him from papers and magazines to keep him up to date.

Often a controversial figure, Archbishop Rummel ordered signs, "FOR COLORED ONLY," removed from Catholic pews. That was almost a decade ago. Again and again he has insisted that there should be no segregation at the communion rail or in church gatherings.

A year before the Supreme Court decision on schools, Archbishop Rummel had already moved against segregation in a Lenten pastoral letter read from every pulpit in his archdiocese. "Public laws, customs of long standing, regulations and agreements of institutions and between business interests are obstacles not easy to overcome," his letter declared. "But we can do much to aid justice and charity by making segregation disappear in our Catholic church life." Archbishop Rummel has also strongly pushed the enrollment of Negro students in seminaries under him.

The most publicized test of the Archbishop's convictions came in the fall of 1955. This crisis involved a young Roman Catholic priest, the Rev. Gerald Lewis, a pleasant, clean-cut Negro from Panama City, Panama. He teaches mathematics and science in the high school of St. Augustin's Seminary, Bay St. Louis. This Mississippi school has six Negroes in a faculty of eighteen priests, and its student body is also mixed. Father Lewis had conducted services in three or four New Orleans white parishes and for a mixed congregation in Edgard, Louisiana, without incident.

As tempers warmed in the great integration debate, Father Lewis was assigned to a little mission church called St. Cecilia. It is about fifteen miles south of New Orleans in a town significantly named Jesuit Bend, in a territory explored long ago by Jesuit priests.

Shortly after midnight on the morning before he was to say mass, he received a telephone call telling him not to go ahead. Father Lewis shrugged off the warning. But when he came to the little church, he was met outside by a group of parishioners. There was a police car, and he saw two armed men in uniform. The group told him that they didn't want him conducting the services there.

"They were very polite," he reported later. "They informed me that a Negro could not say mass for a white congregation. . . .

"With the police standing there, my first thought was that this was the law laying down a command. I just didn't argue. If I had known they were just a few of the parishioners and a couple of deputies, I might have gone on in the church and said mass anyway."

The priest circumspectly retreated. But his superior, Archbishop Rummel, the champion of integration, was no man to bow before this interference. He moved quickly. He suspended services in the mission church and also cut out one of the three masses at a nearby church, pleading shortage of priests. In a letter to the congregation, he called the parishioners' blockade of the priest "an act of injustice, uncharitableness, and irreverence." It was also, he reminded them, a violation of church law.

"The only reason alleged for this unwarranted interference with the discharge of his duty was the fact that he is a member of the Negro race," Archbishop Rummel charged. "This incident was clearly a violation of the obligation of reverence and devotion which Catholics owe to every priest of God, regardless of race, color, or nationality."

Two days later, the Vatican called the Archbishop's action "prompt, admirable, pastoral, Catholic" but termed the parishioners' acts "sacrilegious." It added: "Racial exclusivism is a sin against the nature of the Catholic creed."

Back in Louisiana, the congregation was quiet only temporarily. Members signed a defiant petition.

"If no white priest is available," they said, "let the church remain closed."

One of the leaders, J. B. Perez, headed a delegation of protest to the Archbishop. He was backed by his brother, Leander H. Perez, a New Orleans lawyer and district attorney and an acknowledged Roman Catholic lay power. Leander Perez asserted, with an approach rather unusual in dealing with Catholic archbishops: "I don't care to discuss the matter because I view it as nothing less than pro-Communist propaganda."

The Jesuit Bend trouble had not quieted down before difficulty broke out not far away in Erath, Louisiana. For several years both Negro and white students here had learned the catechism of basic Roman Catholic principles in the same class. Now two local Catholic women beat a woman teacher who did the instructing.

Promptly Bishop Jules B. Jeanmard inflicted on the pair the strongest Roman Catholic penalty, excommunication, which bars a member from confession and even last rites.

Moreover, the Bishop warned that anyone else who threatened interference with church operations would automatically be excommunicated. If there was another act of violence, he added, the church would be closed. His decree was posted on the front door of the building and read at all masses. Later the proper apologies were made, the excommunication was lifted, and integrated classes were resumed.

An early 1956 statement by Archbishop Rummel that segregation is "morally wrong" was interpreted as meaning the archdiocese's sixty thousand white and twelve thousand Negro students would soon be integrated. This was especially important in New Orleans, where the majority of the schools are parochial. But after segregationists booed his name and burned a cross in his yard, the prelate announced that integration would not begin before September, 1957, "because of certain difficulties."

Roman Catholics who favor the end of school segregation cite with pride the action in St. Louis parochial schools.

When integration was attempted there in 1947, seven hundred Roman Catholic parents, some of them wealthy and influential, organized an injunction to stay the action.

Here, too, the hierarchy acted. Archbishop Joseph E. Ritter firmly reminded them that they would be excommunicated if they interfered with a bishop by recourse to authority outside the church. The opposition folded.

For years now, white and colored Roman Catholic students have mingled happily in the St. Louis parochial schools. One result, a St. Louis Roman Catholic recently claimed, is that the non-Catholic Negro is "turning more and more" to the Roman church.

In Washington, D. C., Archbishop Patrick A. O'Boyle ran into great hostility when he insisted that there should be no discrimination in the church. Even before the Supreme Court decision, he nevertheless started integrating students of all races in parochial schools. The Norfolk, Virginia, Catholic High School is the only integrated school in that city.

For several years, Texas Roman Catholics tried mixed classes in parochial schools, and this worked out satisfactorily. About the time of the court decision, Archbishop Robert E. Lucey of San Antonio announced the banning of racial segregation in schools under him.

In the fall of 1955, leaders of Jesuit High School in Dallas, accepting the first two Negro students of this school, said: "It is our conviction that all citizens of this country should obey the Constitution and the laws as they are interpreted by the Supreme Court. . . . While the decree does not extend to private institutions, its spirit plainly does. Jesuit High School . . . is thoroughly American."

The National Catholic Education Association in 1956 voted to urge the church to lead in school desegregation. A survey by the National Catholic Welfare Conference showed that only six Southern states had taken no steps to integrate Roman Catholic schools; now Archbishop Rummel's moves are reducing that number to five. The Rev. Louis J. Twomey, regent of the law school of Loyola University, New Orleans, predicted that all Roman Catholic schools in the South will be integrated by 1958.

¶Let's Look at the Record

Looking back, many Roman Catholics feel that they missed their opportunity to win large numbers of Negroes after the War Between the States. Only about one per cent of the seven million Negroes in the nation at that time were Roman Catholics, most of them in Maryland and Louisiana. Bishops in a plenary council discussed the freed Negro, but produced no concrete plan for mission work. Then for decades the church was busy with masses of immigrants. Separate churches for Negroes sprang up, especially after World War I. In 1944 Myrdal reported that the Negroes were allowed to attend white Roman Catholic churches only in southern Louisiana, the section influenced by French and Creole tradition—and the area, ironically enough, where the recent sparks have flared. But segregation has been the dominant pattern. Only a third of Negro Roman Catholics are in mixed churches. (Roman Catholic interracial leaders, who say that many conversions have brought the total of Negro Roman Catholics to half a million, set the number of unchurched Negroes at seven million, the number of Protestant Negroes at seven and a half million.)

During the last century, Roman Catholicism can nevertheless point to several examples of successful racial activity. Seventy-two Negroes became priests. Perhaps the most significant of them all was James Augustine Healy, the first Negro priest as well as the first and only Negro Roman Catholic prelate in this country.

Jim Healy was the oldest of ten children of a mulatto slave girl who was married to an Irish planter in Georgia—a marriage that was valid to the church, though a violation of state law. As a young priest in 1854, Father Healy became secretary to the Bishop of Boston. At twenty-five, he was chancellor of the diocese. When he finished twenty years of service in Boston, he was rector of the cathedral.

In 1875, still only forty-five, he became bishop at Portland, Maine. Anti-Catholic Yankees and some of his own flock disparaged him as "the Nigger Bishop," but poor Irish immigrants called him "the Bishop of the poor." He visited his parishes by stagecoach and buggy, and he required all priests to learn French so that they could care for French-Canadians of the diocese. Shortly before his death in 1900, Bishop Healy stipulated that he should be robed in very plain vestments and buried in a simple wooden coffin. His life ended, as it began, in humble simplicity.

One important factor pushing American Roman Catholics toward racial tolerance is the position of the Pope. The Vatican has traditionally frowned on having separate schools, according to *Catholic Digest*, and the permission was given only until American customs changed.

¶The Roman Catholics Organize Interracially

Several interracial movements have blossomed within Roman Catholicism. One of the most significant is the Catholic Committee of the South. It was started by a small but vocal group of Southern Roman Catholics meeting at Cleveland in 1939 beneath a Confederate flag used in the War Between the States. Priests, nuns, and lay leaders cooperate in this committee, and its board includes the archbishops and bishops of Southern dioceses.

On the church front, the CCS has worked for integration of parish societies and urged that all religious processions be interracial. Outside the church, it seeks public acceptance of interracial personnel and nonsegregation of patients in Southern hospitals. Not long ago the Rev. Joseph

H. Fichter, S.J., founder of the Commission on Human Rights of the CCS, declared that this commission's objective is the complete integration of Roman Catholics in parish activities, schools, and city church organizations, without regard to race.

Another significant Roman Catholic movement is that of the Friendship Houses. Not long before CCS was started, a Russian immigrant noblewoman, Baroness Catherine de Hueck, decided personally to help the Negroes near her, and rented a cramped, cold-water flat in Harlem. In this first Friendship House, she and her followers began to fight for Negro rights, protesting evictions, helping find jobs, giving day care to slum children, and getting sick Negroes into hospitals.

There are now Friendship Houses also in Chicago, Washington, and Portland, Oregon. The staffs are interracial. Members volunteer for at least a year at $6 a month, and they get room and board in a tenement above the Friendship House itself or nearby. They eat the simplest meals and wear the castoffs donated for distribution to the poor.

The Friendship House credo is: "As long as a Negro in America is not treated as a brother in Christ and a child of our Father in Heaven, not given due recognition of his dignity as a man . . . *Friendship House has work to do.*"

A third important Roman Catholic movement is closely linked to the name of the Rev. John LaFarge, an editor on *America,* the Jesuit weekly. He is a member of a prominent artistic family; his father was John LaFarge, a noted muralist, and one of his brothers is a well-known architect.

Now in his late seventies, Father LaFarge has an unruly

lock of not-so-gray hair that dips over his forehead and gives him a youthful look belying his slight stoop. In 1955 he celebrated his double jubilee, having been both priest and Jesuit for fifty years. Ordained in Austria in 1905, he had entered the Society of Jesus in Poughkeepsie, New York, and later served as a missionary among Negroes in Maryland for many years.

Father LaFarge founded the Catholic Interracial Council in New York in 1934. Today there are twenty-four of these councils, seven in the South.

The Roman Catholic hierarchy's attitude toward the movement was revealed when the Knights of Columbus refused a charter to an interracial council in Cleveland. Auxiliary Bishop Floyd L. Begin cracked down, told the Knights to stop dragging their feet. "They should grant a charter and be done with it," he said, "and not inquire about the color of members' skins. . . . Either I have to say Negroes are second-rate Catholics, or I must say Knights are not acting as Catholics. The decision is obvious."

Father LaFarge has also tackled the Knights. Urging Northerners to drop their own prejudice before castigating the South, he cited the Knights as an example of Northern prejudice. Few of their councils admit Negroes, he declared —but one of the first that did was in San Antonio!

Undergirding the interracial councils is a succinct view of Christianity expressed several years ago by *America*: "It cannot be too strongly emphasized that racial segregation is a moral question; in plain words, that it is a grave sin, just as adultery and murder are grave sins."

In a recent article, Father LaFarge declared that religion's best weapon today is application of Christianity to all, and "the most important field for realizing this idea is the interracial parish." The segregated parish is not a solution. There is a "deadly ambiguity" every time a Negro Catholic moves in a city. "The ambiguity can be removed only when all members of the parish, *in all that pertains to the parish*, unite in wholehearted cooperation and equality."

Sometimes, he wrote, the interracial parish has been started deliberately; sometimes it has resulted when a white neighborhood has been "invaded."

"The pastor in such a case can tolerate this change as a calamity, patiently doing the best he can under the circumstances," he declared. "Or he can regard it as a God-given opportunity to prove right the Church's mission program to the world. Thank God that so many Catholic pastors in this country today are of this latter category!" [1]

¶The Story of a Virginian

At Newton Grove, a little place of 450 in North Carolina, there were two frame Roman Catholic churches. Some 350 white persons belonged to one. Ninety Negroes belonged to the other. The churches were segregated.

In the spring of 1953, the young, sharp-eyed Bishop of Raleigh, Vincent S. Waters—himself a native of Virginia—decided the time to end church segregation had come. Two years before he had hinted it must end, and now he simply ordered the two Newton Grove churches to unite. On the last Sunday in May, Bishop Waters himself showed up to say mass for the union. He had three services, but few

[1] *Jubilee*, September, 1955. Used by permission.

came. Negroes outnumbered whites two to one at the first mass. Nine Negroes and three whites came to the second. Twelve Catholics, all white, attended the third.

Segregation is a product of darkness, the Bishop preached to those who would listen. Meantime, an angry mob of parishioners stalked around outside. Some hurled stones against the building.

A plump white woman in blue came out after one of the services and observed, "We've all got to die sometime. Me and them, too." Perhaps a religious sense of man's littleness in a vast universe had made skin color seem unimportant to her during the worship.

But someone in the crowd shouted, "She's crazy."

Leaders of the mob demanded to talk with the Bishop after his third mass. He agreed, provided they came two at a time. Two priests who attempted to control the crowd pushing toward the door were manhandled. The Bishop did talk with the protesters—but he did not retreat.

The next month, Bishop Waters moved again. He ended racial segregation in all the churches of the Raleigh diocese (there are twenty-eight thousand Roman Catholics in North Carolina). In a letter to his people, he described Christian duties in a way that may spur Protestants, too:

The Church does not propose tolerance which is negative, but love which is positive. . . . These (Negroes) are our friends and members of our own body, the Church. It is our duty, as Christians of the early days, not only to love them but to serve them, to help them. . . . All of this presupposes the right to worship God freely with us.

4 CAN THE RACES BE INTEGRATED IN THE CHURCH?

IKE MANY ANOTHER PROTESTANT
pastor, young Henry A. Buchanan felt he had
to make a moral decision when the Supreme
Court outlawed segregation in the public
schools. He thought it over, then told his Baptist congregation at Shellman, Georgia: "The
unpleasant truth is that the Supreme Court has
rendered a just decision, and we must accept it
simply because it is right."

His talk disturbed the Shellman Baptists.
Some wanted to fire him. The members first
voted to keep him; then, reversing, decided,
seventy-eight to seventeen, that they should
look for a new pastor.

Young Baptist Buchanan left in incandescent indignation. The town, he recommended,

should "secede from the United States." And sounding a bit
like an old prophet, he declared hotly: "I shake the dust of
Shellman from my feet!"

Thus one group of Protestants reacted to the meaning of
the court decision. Others felt that it challenged the churches
as well as the schools to become interracial. Many had already taken a stand on segregation within the church. For
example, there was a deacon at Marble Collegiate, the New
York church of Dr. Norman Vincent Peale. In an article in
Life, Dr. Peale was quoted as describing how this businessman reacted when the question of admitting a Negro to
membership in the church first came up (there are now a
good many in this church). The deacon settled the matter
for the group with a brimstone-scorched exclamation and
the belligerent demand, "It's a Christian church, isn't it?"

This salty layman put bluntly what the church has been
saying at its highest levels. Churches have often declared
there should be integration in the schools, as we have seen
in Chapter 2; they have also asked for integration in the
church itself. Not only the National Council of Churches,
but also national bodies of twenty communions have in the
last decade endorsed an inclusive ministry to all, regardless of color. At Evanston shortly after the court decision on
schools, the World Council of Churches assembly urged
members "to renounce all forms of segregation."

Church editors pressed for action. The Baptist *Missions*
pointed out that, paradoxically, integration was coming
more slowly in the churches than elsewhere and asked: "Is
it not about time that we do something to speed up the
process?" G. Elson Ruff, editor of *The Lutheran*, warned

that church members would be tempted to steer around non-white prospects during the Lutherans' new evangelism drive. "I doubt if we can expect divine blessing on our efforts unless we start with determination to recognize no limitations on our assignment," he wrote. "If we fail in this, we may be fairly accused of wishing merely to build up our churches as private institutions, not as the household of God."

The Northern Presbyterians started a church-wide Operation Desegregation to attack discrimination in every area of church life. In Richmond, Virginia, Southern Presbyterians in 1955 elected as moderator the antisegregationist president of a Georgia seminary that accepts Negro day students. Then, by a 293 to 109 vote, they reiterated a stand against segregation (the 1954 vote: 236 to 169). The Episcopal Diocesan Convention of New Jersey decreed integration in all parishes. White Methodist women of Mississippi, meeting at Jackson, adopted a charter proposing that "local societies and guilds should give increased emphasis to the working together of all racial groups."

But there were dissenters. For example, Mrs. Sam U. Smith, leader of a faction opposed to the Mississippi Methodist women's position, said that "everyone can see this will lead to complete integration"; she urged women to declare, "We have gone far enough." More than two hundred Methodists from five Southern states met in Birmingham to fight church integration. The host pastor, Dr. Guy B. McGowen, said, "We note with exceeding grave concern efforts being made within our church for sudden and drastic changes . . . in social relationships between the races on the congregational level."

In North Carolina, an Episcopal minister declared that the integrationists really aim for a racial amalgamation "abhorrent" to God. A Brookfield, Illinois, man charged *Presbyterian Life:* "You are furthering and abetting the Communist Manifesto of mixing the races."

However, knowing Protestants pointed out that few whites or Negroes desire to marry into the other race. Considerable race mixing occurred during slave days, but sociologists report that racial intermarriage in states with integrated schools is "statistically insignificant." Church integrationists believe the intermarriage argument begs the question.

¶The Color Line Against Its Background

These differing Christian views of integration have roots that run back deep into the slave system and early American history.

In colonial days slaves were owned in the North as well as the South. Already in the late 1600's, Quakers had begun protesting against slaveholding. A most effective early fighter against slavery was Dr. Samuel Hopkins, a Congregational pastor in Newport, Rhode Island. This was a center of slave trading, and his preaching made him widely disliked; one wealthy family left his church. In the 1780's, Baptists in Virginia and Kentucky came out against slavery. When the Methodist Episcopal Church was formed in 1784, the founders adopted a rule that every slaveholding member must free his slaves within a year.

Then the cotton gin was invented. Slavery's tentacles got new life and spread through the cottonland. By 1832, two Congregational pastors, Dr. Lyman Beecher and Dr. Leonard Bacon, were founding the American Anti-Slavery Society.

A few years later, Baptists in the South felt they must protest the antislavery actions of their "meddlesome" Northern brethen. A Georgia request that a slaveholder be named a home missionary was turned down by the home board. The upshot was that in 1845 Baptists of eight slaveholding states separated from the Northern Baptists. Meantime the Methodists, disagreeing over suspension of a slaveholding minister in Baltimore, also decided to separate, and division came which ended only in 1939. Not long after, slavery also split the Presbyterians.

So church after church divided, a century and more ago, because of differing views. Church historian William Warren Sweet concludes: "There are good arguments to support the claim that the split in the churches was not only the first break between the sections, but the chief cause of the final break."

What became of the Negro meantime? At first, many slaveholders had opposed Christianizing the slaves, lest baptism be interpreted as a sign they should be freed. Later some slaveowners let Negroes attend and sit in separate sections of white churches. But by the end of the War Between the States, few Negroes—perhaps only one in six —were Christians. The myth of the religiosity of the Negro had not yet well started.

Only now did evangelism among Negroes really get going, and the Negro churches, some of which had existed over half a century, began to grow. If the segregated church seems to have existed forever, it should be recalled that it has developed largely in the last seventy-five years, during the lifetime of some now alive. The tradition of the segregated church belongs essentially to only the latter *fourth* of the long period of American history since Jamestown was settled in 1607.

Today the Negro denominations are well established, with more than 90 per cent of Negro membership, and whites who do not want mixed churches are close to the truth when they say that many Negroes prefer to have their own churches. Within the framework of their own churches, Negroes can enjoy the freedom and equality that they cannot ordinarily feel in white society. The Negro church is an important center of the segregated life in unofficial ghettos. Here the Negro is not forever under white domination but is under Negro leadership. Here the Negro can develop into a leader himself; it is not a mere coincidence that Congressman A. Clayton Powell, onetime New York City councilman and newspaper publisher, was first the Rev. A. Clayton Powell of the great Abyssinian Baptist Church in Harlem.

Sometimes the segregated Negro church is unfriendly to whites. However, Negro churches are no more necessarily anti-white than white churches are anti-Negro. One of the best-known Negro churches has taken the trouble to make this explicit. With five thousand attending a conference in Texas, the African Methodist Episcopal Church declared it is not exclusively Negro: "People of all races have always been welcome in our churches. Our denomination was organized as a protest against discrimination. With this in mind, we urge you to be more forceful in spreading information to the world that our membership is not limited by color, class, or caste."

Not the least of the problems of desegregation is dealing with the momentum of denominations that are essentially Negro and with the Negro work of white churches.

Some Negro leaders naturally caution against too great haste in desegregating. For example, L. B. Tinsley, leader of the Colored Cumberland Presbyterian Church, apologized to the Cumberland denomination because a proposal for a white executive secretary could not be approved.

"Knowing our people as we do," he explained, "we feel that more time is needed in order to prepare our membership for such a venture." Until Negroes are better accepted as leaders in the white church, there appears little reason for them to be hasty in turning over their own leadership to whites.

Declaring that he spoke for his entire church, Bishop H. B. Shaw of the African Methodist Episcopal Zion Church asserted in 1956 that the identity of the Negro church must not "be lost in the shuffle of integration."

Meantime, segregated work expands in some places. The Southern Presbyterians, for example, had a two million dollar campaign for work among Negroes. The fund was used to construct several Negro churches and build up a Negro college.

So new habits are formed, new leaders developed, new traditions begun—all in the old segregated patterns.

On the other hand, the only Negro congregation of the American Lutheran Church in the Pacific Northwest was disbanded in 1955. All members of this Portland, Oregon, church received written invitations to unite with white churches of the city. The Rev. S. C. Siefkes, the church's district president, said: "It is the first time I have dissolved a congregation, and I feel it is a victory."

¶What Are the Interracial Possibilities?

For many years, Protestants have felt that they should do something about breaking down the color lines within the church. Hundreds of churches have arranged for Negro and white ministers to exchange pulpits, and white youth have sometimes visited Negro churches.

From time to time, a headline has reminded the North that Christians in the South have also been pioneering. Such a headline blossomed when twenty-five Negro delegates from the Congregational Christian Southern Convention met in Alabama with twenty-five white delegates of the Southeast Convention. A group of hoodlums arrived as the group was at worship in a chapel, and the leader shouted, "We'll give you thirty minutes to get those niggers out of there." The Negroes left before the gang returned. But perhaps the more significant fact is that many such interracial groups meet unmolested.

Writing in *The New York Times Magazine*, Hodding Carter of Greenville, Mississippi, cited the church as one place where segregation is breaking down.

"My white fellow townsmen took quite calmly the fact that . . . Negro delegates to a state-wide convocation in Greenville of a Protestant denomination dined in the church annex with the rest of the delegates and were served by the women of the church," he wrote.

The moral pressure is always for more and more fellow-ship. Speaking of a typical young Mississippi Negro, Carter said that "he is questioning the Christianity of white South-erners who don't want Negroes to study in the same theo-logical schools with white divinity students nor to worship in the same churches."

Mrs. Sarah Patton Boyle, a faculty wife at the University of Virginia, told similarly in *The Saturday Evening Post* of interracial church activities in Charlottesville. The local paper will not use Mr., Mrs., and Miss with the names of Negroes who help on these projects, she reported, so white church groups sometimes refuse to put out publicity on them. Like Carter's young Negro, Mrs. Boyle said she be-lieves that Christianity requires that Negroes and whites be permitted to worship together.

"I've just heard something horrible," a friend once told Mrs. Boyle. "Our minister warned us that within a few years we can expect to have Negroes in our church!"

But this friend began to grow more tolerant with ex-perience and before long she told some of her acquaintances that she had met two Negro women and thought they were very nice!

So, hesitantly, the churches throughout America begin to face up to the possibility of the "mixed" church. But are they ready to move from mild interracial experiments on to the integrated congregation?

"Yes," say some. But studies indicate that many churches are still pondering.

The Minnesota poll, conducted by *The Minneapolis Trib-une*, found that 77 per cent of the men and women in that state are in favor of having white and Negro people "worshiping together in the same churches."

A survey of 137 churches in the Presbytery of Pittsburgh revealed that thirteen are interracial in membership and another twenty-nine have interracial participation; more than half of the segregated churches said that a majority of their members favor integration.

A study made for the Church Federation of Greater Dayton, Ohio, showed that its churches are lagging behind industry and the schools in integrating the races. Only one white church of 120 has Negro members. Seven white churches have moved from the Negro housing area and—the study summarized sadly—Dayton churches are dying in the midst of very dense populations. As home mission experts emphasize, such is the fate of the downtown church in many communities unless it decides for integration.

Pittsburgh, with one interracial church in ten, appears to be more typical than Dayton. The Disciples of Christ, in a nationwide survey, got replies from 2,051 churches. Of these, 261—more than 10 per cent—reported they now have members other than white. (This would include not only Negroes but also Indians, Japanese-Americans, and perhaps foreign students.) Another 114 churches said members of nonwhite races attend, and forty-three others said that they would welcome persons of other races.

Significantly, among the states in which nonwhite members are in Disciples churches were California, Florida, Georgia, Louisiana, North and South Carolina, and Virginia; in Texas, twenty-two Disciples churches reported members of more than one race.

The Northern Baptists found that in each of twenty-eight states one or more of their congregations have Negro members. Chinese, Japanese, and American Indian members were reported also in many churches. The Baptists "are well along the path to putting first things first," concludes Bernice Cofer, secretary of the denomination's Department of Christian Friendliness.

The most extensive research on integration was undertaken jointly by the United Lutherans, Congregational Christians, and Presbyterians (U.S.A.). They found that 1,331 out of 13,597 predominantly white churches have nonwhite members or attenders. That is just short of 10 per cent. Of the racially inclusive churches, forty-five were in the Southeastern region of the United States, the Deep South.

Did not this integration cause great disruption? No, only about *one in ten thousand* left the integrating churches— twenty-six individuals, in fact, out of 237,000 church members.

"The average American church member is not opposed to racially inclusive congregations either in theory or in practice," a National Council of Churches news release stated. "And when actually confronted with a real situation involving racial integration, church members generally behave in a way superior to what they themselves have anticipated."

In every instance of appraisal after a member left because of the race question, the ministers found in the congregation an increased spiritual insight. Fellowship was warmer, dedication greater.

Reporting on their part of the survey, the Presbyterians

said they learned that 433 churches out of 2,706 have non-white members. But their statistics showed also that the inclusiveness had not gone very far. More than three fourths of the 433 churches had fewer than five nonwhite members. Only thirty-seven had ten or more. This also proves, incidentally, that when Negroes begin to join a church, they do not automatically take it over. Preachers have just as much trouble getting Negroes to be Christians as they have getting whites!

When prejudice is so widespread, how can white congregations be persuaded to admit even a few?

The Presbyterians' answer is that majority approval beforehand is not necessary. A special issue of the denomination's magazine, *Social Progress*, points out why.[1] Changes in attitudes come most easily when the social situation changes. The way people act can change before they say they are willing to change. That is, members will mostly go along and adjust to the idea of attending church together with Negroes when it just comes naturally. This is true even though they might think beforehand that they would dislike the idea.

A pastor explained: "Since race prejudice is rooted in the emotions rather than in the intellect, rational arguments against it are futile. But few people, even the most prejudiced, can fail to grow and change when they share the deep experience of worship and friendship in the church with persons of another race."

---

[1] This special edition, "Segregation on Sunday" (January, 1955), is an excellent practical guide to desegregation in the local church. *Social Progress* is published at 830 Witherspoon Building, Philadelphia 7, Pa.

Again and again, the Presbyterians have found that the pastor and one to four laymen—a "cell of the concerned"—were enough to make congregations "fully Christian in their practice of racial and cultural inclusiveness." It is the leaven idea working again, even within the body of the church.

"That's all very well in theory," someone objects. "But I'd have to be shown how it worked out in real practice."

Well, here is the way it went in one place.

¶Case History in Detroit

The story of how integration came to a Michigan church is told by the pastor who was instrumental in the change, the Rev. H. B. Sissel. Now associate secretary of the Presbyterian Department of Social Education and Action, Mr. Sissel recalled how he went to St. Andrew's parish in Detroit in 1949, fresh out of seminary. The church was dying. For three or four years, Negroes had been moving in around it, and whites were leaving in panic. Attendance was down to 175 and sometimes less, in spite of a membership of 460. Mr. Sissel decided that the church should not move but stay put and that therefore it would have to serve the changing community.

"I was able to discover two or three committed Christians who were dedicated to the task," Mr. Sissel said. Members of this little group decided that they would try to make the church inclusive. That is, they would take Negroes. But they would avoid speculation and argument. They would keep discussion on the level of the personal responsibility of each member to act like a Christian.

They also decided not to try to get a resolution passed. In

the first place, resolving to admit Negroes would be "to create and then remove a prohibition that does not exist," since membership in the church is by profession of faith in Jesus Christ. Also, a vote would have drawn battle lines and divided the congregation.

During the campaign, Mr. Sissel drove around and noted down the addresses with "For Sale" signs. Later, he visited the families that moved into these houses and invited them to church. He also preached a sermon on race relations. The church had Negro speakers at women's meetings. There was a pulpit exchange.

One day a member came to the pastor after Sunday service with a question. He was one who had leaned toward ending segregation but was unsure. Now he said a Negro family had moved into his block. What should he do?

What, asked the pastor, would he do if it were a white family?

He'd ask them to church.

"Well," said the pastor, putting it up to the man's conscience, "you decide what you should do about this family."

The man first brought the Negro children to Sunday school with his own. Then he and his wife brought the mother to church with them. When the first three Negroes were later admitted to membership, she was one of them. This was only about nine months after Mr. Sissel had become pastor of the church.

The Presbyterian session was informed meantime about developments. There was some questioning, but a strong Christian elder spoke about the responsibility of the church to receive all, and that established a favorable atmosphere.

Curiously enough, however, the man who had brought his Negro neighbor and her children was punished. He was put up for the eldership by the nominating committee, but competition arose.

"For the first time in the history of the church, a nomination was made from the floor, and this man was defeated in the election," explained the pastor. "There was no question in the mind of anyone as to the reason for his defeat. . . . The man who was defeated had in effect committed ecclesiastical suicide by acting upon his Christian convictions."

Meantime, Negro children were coming to Sunday school. Two or three qualified Negro members became teachers. One or two joined the choir. On a Laymen's Sunday, one Negro member participated in conduct of the worship service.

This last was the final straw for one member, who resigned and took his wife to another white church. But theirs was one of the few defections.

"To my knowledge," Mr. Sissel said, "only about two or three families left the church directly as a result of Negroes' being received into membership."

The overall effect was revitalizing. During the four years of Mr. Sissel's pastorate, 150 were taken into the church—90 per cent of them on confession of faith. The first year after the Rev. Malcolm B. Sylvester succeeded him, more than fifty additional were received. The congregational ratio is about three Negro members to ten white. The church complexion, in other words, is close to that of the community in which it stands.

"A new solidarity, sense of mission, and optimism gradually could be sensed," Mr. Sissel recalled. "In the case of
perhaps seven or ten individuals, radical changes in their
conception of the Christian faith and in their sense of
dedication resulted from their new experience of Christian
fellowship at a deeper level."

Isn't the experience of this Detroit church exceptional?

No. We turn now to a number of cases that indicate it
is rather a typical experience for churches that dare to
pioneer.

5 INTEGRATION: NO LONGER AN EXPERIMENT

IT ALL STARTED, FITTINGLY ENOUGH, with a Good Samaritan deed. In wintry South Chicago, a new young minister named Johnson was helping push a car out of a snowbank. The engine raced, the wheels spun, and the pastor puffed; slowly the car crawled through. Then the driver climbed out to say thanks.

The minister chatted with her, and since she lived near, he ended by inviting her to come to church on Sunday. She did.

So began the integration of one of Chicago's several remarkable interracial churches. That automobile driver, Mrs. Render Gray, principal of an elementary school, became the first Negro from the neighborhood to sit in the pews of the all-white, eighty-five-year-old Salem Augustana Lutheran Church. Not long after, her niece and nephew were welcomed at Sunday school. Other children followed; and today the skin-deep line of color has been wiped out by Christian friendship at Salem.

It was not the first time that the Rev. Philip A. Johnson and his attractive young wife had met the race problem. During World War II, in a Riverside, California, parish, they had taken into their home a young Japanese girl, so that she could finish her education instead of going to a reloca-tion center. They were moved by her firsthand information about how it feels to be a member of an unwanted minority.

In 1949 they went to the Salem Church on Chicago's South Side, in the Cottage Grove section. About the same time, the first Negro family came into this all-white area, and violence broke out. Chicago was peppered with hate pamphlets, bombs, house-burnings, and headlines. This neighborhood appeared to have no leaders nor organization to maintain sanity.

Pastor Johnson got the mimeograph busy and started put-ting out letters to the residents. "To gather in crowds can do no possible good," he said in one message. "To sell our homes in panic is to lose our investment in them. Fair play is the American and the Christian way."

The minister also tried to organize his colleagues in the other churches. "How far we are from the kingdom of God!" one neighbor pastor wrote him in disappointment. Other church leaders despaired, especially when roving gangs of White Circle Leaguers intimidated those who came to meet-ings called by Pastor Johnson.

The crisis began to take its toll. Some churches merged

with distant white congregations. Four ministers and a priest collapsed with heart attacks or nervous breakdowns. Of eight white Protestant churches in the area, two moved out, three died or merged.

But Pastor Johnson visited in homes to talk about what Christianity has to say on race issues, wrote strong editorials in the church paper, and preached sermons on tolerance.

"In those days of tension," Johnson recalls, "a Biblical text on brotherhood would hit out across the assembled congregation like a whiplash."

Some members came along, but many were slow in giving up their fears. Those first two years, attendance slumped.

"It was strange," the minister says now. "Some of the members I interviewed said to me, 'I agree with you, Pastor. I know that you are acting according to God's word. But I can't go along with you. I am not that strong. I will have to move out of the community.'"

Then church attendance began to pick up. In 1952, Mr. Johnson tallied up the score. He found that Salem had lost sixty-two members—but only a third of those because of the race dispute. However, it had picked up sixty-two; thirty-eight of these were Negroes, twenty-four white. The church was becoming genuinely interracial. By 1954, attendance was back up to the number it had been before a Negro moved into the neighborhood, and it was still going up. In 1955 it was 650, including ninety Negroes.

Has such a strong dose of Christianity been hard on finances? No. During World War II, the average pledge was $32. Now it was up to $140—almost $3 a person each Sunday.

"There are only nineteen confirmed members of the church, including high school students, who give less than fifty cents per Sunday," says the pastor.

Today, there is multiracial participation in the women's federation, Luther Leagues, and other groups. This congregation works also for better race relations outside its walls. Members press the Real Estate Board, for example, to control agents who incite residents to sell. "By working together," members remind such salesmen, "we can maintain the standards we want and enjoy cultural advantages and pleasant relationships."

What does Pastor Johnson, in retrospect, feel Christians should do when they contemplate taking in Negroes? Here are some of his answers:

Think of an unchurched minority-group person as an opportunity for intelligent Christian witness, not as a problem.

Avoid compromising the gospel or church to suit prejudices.

Be clear on the implications of the gospel—that Christ is for *all* men, without distinction.

Be friendly, never patronizing.

¶Case Study in Methodism

Not far from Salem, in the exclusive South Shore district, is Methodism's cathedral church, St. James. It is the denomination's largest and finest church plant in Chicago.

With World War II, the St. James area changed, became 85 per cent colored. Children abounded; there were more than five thousand grade-school pupils within a mile of the church. But St. James was becoming a shell. Its Sunday school dwindled to twenty-five—or *one for every three* rooms in the gigantic parish house!

In July, 1953, Bishop Charles W. Brashares assigned the Rev. E. Jerry Walker to St. James. "Whatever happens," the Bishop told him, "even if the church closes its doors in six months' time, we'll stand behind you."

"It was," Mr. Walker recalls, "the hardest assignment I ever faced."

The wife of a prominent member told the minister that if he "insisted on any foolishness, such as 'mixing the races' in church," so many pledges would be canceled so fast the church would die on the spot.

Jerry Walker ignored the free advice and decided to start with the children. First he offered the church recreational facilities to the YMCA if the "Y" would provide a program. A part-time director was immediately assigned. Church members took obvious pride in this step. However, when Mr. Walker proposed an interracial Sunday school, several canceled pledges. A few transferred their memberships.

"He's giving our church to the colored," one woman protested indignantly.

But the majority of the church officials stuck by him. Mr. Walker applied to the Chicago Church Federation for aid, seminary students were recruited to teach, and a group of interested mothers began to ring doorbells and invite children.

"We set a goal of 150 pupils for that first eight-week trial period in May and June of 1954," says the minister. "By the second Sunday we had passed our goal."

Meantime, the preacher was squarely up against the problem of adult Negro memberships. Barely two months after he had come, Silas Brown applied for membership. Fine—except that Silas Brown was a Negro. This might upset things. The new minister temporized. Would Mr. Brown mind waiting a bit?

Silas Brown was "a big man"; he kept coming, and in due course he was permitted to join the church. In the fall of 1954, only a little more than a year after Mr. Walker's arrival, seven Negroes and seven whites became members in this "handsome Gothic building provided by some of the city's first families," as the press put it.

"We think it's the Christian thing to do," the pastor told reporters.

Earlier that fall at a board meeting Mr. Walker had pulled from his pocket a list of names of prospective Negro members and asked what to do with it.

"That was when a most remarkable thing happened," he recalls. "I guess you would call it a sort of testimonial meeting."

A woman who had been planning to move out of the community said she would stay and help. A man who had said he was leaving for good if any Negroes sat in his pew declared, "I'm going to do my part to see this through."

A retired Pullman executive confessed: "Five years ago I refused to shake hands with a Negro on one of our trains. I'm ashamed of it. Let's do what is right and do it now!"

"I want to be the first to welcome our new members," asserted a trustee who had been urging that the church sell out. "It's the only Christian thing to do!"

"Well," summarizes Jerry Walker, "We've had a rebirth—

a Christian experience. And interestingly enough, our growing congregation today includes more white people than
there were in the whole congregation in 1954."

The stories of success with integration at Salem Lutheran
and St. James Methodist do not, of course, indicate that all
Chicago churches are equally imaginative. Many are still
lily-white. Yet Francis McPeak, of the Mayor's Commission
on Human Relations, estimates that there are twenty to
thirty Chicago churches with some degree of integration.

¶Lutherans Leading the Way

What has been happening in Chicago has been happening in many other communities around America, and in
several denominations. Take the Lutherans, for example.

"Dozens of our congregations have received Negro members this past year for the first time," Elson Ruff, editor of
The Lutheran, wrote in May, 1955. Not only that, said Dr.
H. Conrad Hoyer, of the National Lutheran Council, but
"dozens of others are ready to receive them, and many others
have started the educational process to prepare their people
for the day."

In 1953, the Augsburg Lutheran Church in Detroit had
to be torn down to make way for a new expressway. A
majority of members decided to shift the church to the
suburbs, but some chose to stay and build a new interracial
congregation. In June, 1954, they organized it, and on the
first day, eight Negro children and two white were baptized.
The congregation began in a rent-free union hall, but already it has started building.

Home mission boards often support such ventures, and

the United Lutheran Church Board of American Missions agreed to help this church on condition it would accept all who came, regardless of race or background. It has done just that. Not only Negroes and whites but Japanese and Indians belong. Two Negroes were elected to the first church council, and a Negro heads the music and worship committee. In the congregation is an Indian American princess —daughter of a chief—who is married to a Negro lawyer. Both she and her husband sing in the choir.

A slim white man, the Rev. Richard I. Knudsen, is pastor. Formerly professor of church history at Howard University, he was already well versed on race questions.

"We believe that we are pioneering the pattern of the future church," he says. "Our aim is a really open church with arms outspread to embrace every poor and unself-righteous sinner who needs it, regardless of hue of skin."

White members of this church typically comment: "A year ago we would not have dreamed of associating with Negro families. We would have rejected the idea of having them in our homes for a church meeting and eating with them. But today that is all different. We find them wonderful friends."

In the New York metropolitan area, there are several interracial Lutheran churches.

Originally organized for a Swedish immigrant group in 1889, St. Paul Lutheran Church of Brooklyn found its families moving far out on Long Island. In 1951, the congregation voted not to relocate but to try to serve the neighborhood. That meant serving the Negroes who had moved in. Significantly, this sound mission step was taken when the church didn't even have a pastor. The congregation found its "salvation written in black and white," said the Rev. Kenneth W. Dugan, who became its minister; and he added: "We have an Irish pastor leading an interracial congregation originally organized for Swedes!"

The church members went out to visit the homes in the community to invite neighbors to come. Sometimes doors were opened to them, often they were not. The Lutherans began to realize that colored people must be won like anyone else.

"This proved to be something of a surprise to some of the members who had had reservations," reported Pastor Dugan. "These people had expected an immediate influx of Negroes who would take over the church."

There was no influx, but two or three began to attend. After a year there were a dozen Negro members.

As interest grew, members persevered in friendliness. Since many of the new visitors have never been to a Lutheran church, a member always sits with each newcomer and helps him follow the service.

Naturally, this helps impress upon visitors the idea that the welcome is sincere.

Not far from this Brooklyn church is St. Mark Lutheran Church, in a onetime German section of South Jamaica, now largely settled by low-income Negroes. In 1946, a young seminary student named Arnold J. Dahlquist visited the church for the first time, noted how run-down it was, and learned that 90 per cent of its members lived far away. Yet he finally agreed to accept a call to it.

What course should the church follow? He could help it

relocate, urge members to join other churches, or try to
lead the people "in a forthright recognition of the missionary
purpose of the church at home as well as abroad." After
weeks of struggle, young Arnold Dahlquist chose the third
alternative.

"It was the only one which had justification in the Christian faith," he explains simply.

The minister took a "positive, unequivocal, determined
stand" in his preaching. He discussed race in conversations.
Always he avoided getting involved in arguments on real
estate, intermarriage, and other so-called realistic excuses
for segregation. He kept at the fore his belief that discrimination is sin.

"I have clung tenaciously to this one proposition: To refuse relationship with our colored brethren is to turn away
from Jesus Christ," he declares.

After preliminary talks to ascertain attitudes, he chose
four members for a closer test.

"We had a small dinner party at the parsonage at which
a Negro lady was the guest of honor," he recalls. "During
the evening we talked about everything and anything in general, never touching the matter of race relations. My purpose was to determine if these people could accept this
young lady in a social situation and lose consciousness of
color differences.

"The evening was a complete success. Each testified later
that within a short time he had completely forgotten there
was any difference. I knew now I had four people who were
ready to give unqualified assistance."

In vain the pastor tried to get neighborhood youngsters

interested in Sunday school. Discouraged, he prayed, and he believes his prayer was answered.

"God acted. One Sunday a new colored boy in the community, who was of Lutheran background and who set out to find the Lutheran Church (predominantly of Negro membership) some six blocks from us, wandered into our Sunday school. Though he saw only white faces around him, he had the courage to come in and sit down."

Another break followed. A welfare worker told the pastor that he had thirty Protestant children, including a number of Negroes, to send to Sunday school.

Other churches consulted had not agreed to take them without discrimination.

"What's the matter with the Protestant church anyway?" asked this director, an ardent Roman Catholic. "When I consulted the nearby Catholic church, the priest said 'yes' unhesitatingly."

Pastor Dahlquist said "yes," too, and the next Sunday there were suddenly twenty-nine Negro children in his Sunday school!

When the church also added adult Negro members, a few white members left.

"There were some casualties," says the minister. "I think this will always be the case. Some can't stand being Christian beyond the state of profession."

One of the longest experiences with integration is that of another Lutheran church, St. John's in the Bronx. It has been interracial since a quarter of a century ago, when the first steps were taken.

"It was in 1931, when there were few Negroes in the

Bronx," says the present pastor, Alfred J. Schroder. "One Sunday morning a colored Christian mother, who had only recently moved into the neighborhood of St. John's, dressed her three children and sent them to seek a Sunday school. She instructed them to go to whichever church would receive them in a friendly spirit. The children decided to try the big fine church on the hill, St. John's, and they were made welcome. From that moment the course of St. John's was clear."

Pastor Schroder attributes this easy shift to the fact that his predecessors had already made the parishioners "see in every man a child of God, created in the image of God." So there was no serious rupture. Only five families left the church.

Negroes now feel welcome to attend, but the whites keep coming, too. In a recent confirmation class, whites outnumbered Negroes five to one.

"Our proportion of Negroes and whites fluctuates constantly," says the pastor. "At times one third of our Sunday school children are colored; other times, only one fourth. It merely means that we are a truly interracial neighborhood. A person's color means nothing to us."

What about the young people and dating? The minister explains how in a discussion group a young Negro expressed the thoughts of both whites and Negroes about dating across racial lines: "She said it presented problems for the people who attempted it, but more for a new generation. She showed how Negroes as well as whites had a culture and traditions proudly to preserve. And she ended by pointing out that our civilization is not ready for so bold a step. Our young people have formed some fine interracial friendships, but they do not attempt dating across racial lines."

¶*The Presbyterians, Too*

What these Lutheran churches have done has been accomplished also in several other denominations. Let's look at a few case histories, beginning with some from Presbyterian churches.

In the Bronx, the Fort Schuyler Presbyterian Church faced a problem when in 1952 a low-cost public housing project was begun nearby. The Rev. Howard M. Weaving, at an annual meeting of the church, pointed out that the housing expansion would bring many undesirable influences, such as barrooms, which would welcome all patrons, so "the church must certainly exert an ever greater influence."

Here the transition to integration was made with practically no stir.

"We work together, we eat together, certainly we should worship together!" said the elders. "It's character, not color, that counts!"

When the first families moved into the project, the minister trudged through deep snow to welcome them. In time, some Negro newcomers wanted to join the church. The pastor presented the names, making no mention of the applicants' race.

What happened to the budget and attendance this time?

"Since becoming an interracial church, we have for the first time had our budget for current expenses, benevolences, building fund, and so on, totally subscribed by our weekly pledges," says Pastor Weaving. "Our attendance requires double church services and double sessions for Sunday school."

At the First Presbyterian Church of Mount Vernon, New York, another housing project brought a gradual and almost unnoticed change. One Sunday school teacher remarked that her department was a regular United Nations in miniature, including Negroes, Puerto Ricans, Chinese, Japanese, and children from several European nations.

Questions were raised, however, when the possibility arose that some nonwhite adults might actually join the church. Shouldn't Negroes support their own churches? But there was no Negro Presbyterian church in town.

The church had two long meetings lasting until after midnight. Should the congregation put into practice the high-sounding pronouncements of official church bodies?

The meetings were curiously Quakerlike, as the Rev. Melvin J. Joachim, the minister, remembers them: "There were indeed tense moments. But there were also moments of precious calm, such as when prayer was called for. This happened several times. Never was I more confident of the presence of God. And several elders mentioned later that they truly felt the guidance of the Holy Spirit."

No minutes were taken, no resolutions passed. But the sense of the meeting was that all applicants should be examined and trained, without discrimination.

That was about five years ago. What has happened?

"Attendance and finances are the best they have ever been," reports the pastor. "The split in the church that some feared has never occurred. A Negro is teaching in the Sunday school, one sings in the choir, several attend the adult Bible class, one has taught the class. Eight are members of the church. Twice that number attend regularly.

"A few white families have taken their letters to other churches, but to my knowledge, no family has confessed to anyone that its reason for leaving was the race question. People are not proud of their prejudices."

Sometimes, moreover, a strong conscience shows up unexpectedly. This minister got a telephone call from a substantial contributor whose pledge, some had said, might now be canceled.

"This is it!" thought the pastor.

But the big contributor said: "That was the most Christian action the session of our church has ever taken. And what is more, if they had decided otherwise, I am afraid I would have had to withdraw my support and leave!"

An interracial church is not always achieved by a white church's accepting those of other races. Sometimes the reverse happens. That was the way it worked at Bidwell Street Presbyterian Church in Pittsburgh, Pennsylvania, after a white minister, the Rev. Virgil P. Moccia, took the pulpit. He went to this Negro church in 1952 because he had become dissatisfied with "the incompleteness of segregated Christian fellowship." After about a year, however, he became depressed because he saw that he had exchanged one segregated church for another: "Where I was once a white pastor of an all-white congregation, I was now a white pastor of an all-Negro congregation."

When he expressed his concern, the members agreed to work and pray for a racially inclusive church. Within a year, twenty-five white members had been received.

¶Other Denominations as Well

In Ohio, two white churches, the West Cincinnati Presbyterian Church and a Protestant Episcopal church, St. Barnabas, half a block away, cooperated when the neighborhood
became 70 per cent Negro. To survive, they decided that
they must serve the new population. So in 1945, the churches
united, with the Rev. Maurice F. McCrackin and the Rev.
J. Albert Dalton as co-pastors.

These two decided on a strategy of settlement work.
T. T. Clement and Mrs. Helen Lee, both Negroes, were employed to take charge of the program. Soon hundreds of
young people were coming to the St. Barnabas building.
Again and again youngsters led in creating an interracial
fellowship. For example, the white high school group in
the Presbyterian building and the Negro canteen club in the
other building began to invite each other for Sunday exchange meetings.

Negro children started attending a nursery school opened
by Miss Dorothy Ratterman at the church. One morning a
new white youngster, seeing Negro children for the first
time, expressed some fear. The teacher told him it would
wear off. A week later another new white child came and
reacted in the same way.

"Miss Ratterman," said the first boy with great new so-
phistication, "that was the way I felt when I first came, wasn't
it? But I don't now!"

Fearful to go too fast, the ministers provided a mixed
staff for the annual summer camping season but kept the
periods segregated. This policy got them into difficulty with

the girl campers, however, when about ten white teen-agers from one period wanted to go back for the next period, which was for Negroes. That wouldn't be fair to the Negro girls, the ministers objected. But the white teen-agers simply wouldn't listen to "no."

"All ten of them appeared bag and baggage at the bus the following Monday morning," Mr. McCrackin recalls. "We put it up to the Negro girls as to whether they should go. The answer was, 'Sure, let them come.' . . . These girls were telling us what we in our adult wisdom didn't understand— that we should have had the Negro and white children come together from the beginning."

A little child led them at another point. A white six-year-old girl named Happy brought a Negro friend to the primary department and hopefully asked: "Can Junior come?" She was told "yes." But to make sure that he would feel at home, Happy held his hand through the whole opening worship service.

That first Negro child to attend the federated church school became a symbol of the challenge when the adults began to consider integration. One board member asked why this step was being "forced on us now."

"Who forced Junior on you?" another member asked him.

There simply couldn't be an answer to that one. The board voted twelve to two for integration, and barely two years after the federation service, the first three Negroes joined.

"Like most people, Negroes as a group don't rush to church but have to be persuaded to come," says Mr. Mc-Crackin.

"Where there is a movement of a Negro population into an area and a movement of the white population out of it, it is not the minority that stages an invasion but the majority that stages a retreat. Where there is not a retreat, nobody takes over."

In Cleveland, the stimulus toward an interracial congregation came in a unique way to one Evangelical and Reformed church. After the World War II relocation of Japanese, the Hough Avenue Church found many new Oriental neighbors. The church leaders encouraged these Christians of Japanese ancestry to form a fellowship, and in time they merged with the congregation.

When many Negroes began to move into this neighborhood, the church decided that they, too, should be included. As a result, three races today share in the church and its leadership.

The Congregationalists in Milwaukee have also created a congregation of three races in a church that was founded as an expression of the antislavery movement a century ago. "Grand Avenue Congregational Church Welcomes You," this congregation proclaims on an eight-page brochure; and in living up to this slogan, the group determined to accept its first Negro member in 1949. Japanese also belong to this church.

Another famous interracial church of the Congregationalists is Mt. Hollywood in Los Angeles, of which the well-known pacifist, Allan A. Hunter, is pastor. For many years the membership of this church—sometimes called "the United Nations church"—has included Japanese-Americans and Negroes.

Even before World War II, the congregation was interracial, and one of the most touching moments of the war came when one of the young Negroes, in uniform, was asked to speak. On the pulpit were photographs of two white soldiers who had been killed—old friends with whom he had played right through church school and young people's meetings. He started to speak but broke down. Sobbing, he had to quit his attempt.

"That young Negro simply by crying there without apology did more to interpret to us the sorrow of youth and the absurdity of race prejudice than anything that has been said before or since," says Mr. Hunter. "We were all for the moment burned, fused, melted together."

Today that young man is a member of the board of trustees, a deacon, and an usher, and he and his wife—he was married to a Negro girl in the church—have two children in the church school. Negroes and Japanese-Americans also sing in the choir and teach Sunday school, and a cousin of Ralph Bunche is chairman of the Christian Education Committee.

"The process in our church is unspectacular and possibly too gradual, but it seems normal, unforced, uncontrived," says the pastor.

Sometimes attenders stop coming when they realize the church complexion. On the other hand, those who "see what's what" and still join often bring a strong, dynamic quality vital to the church's life. A few years ago a girl from Alabama attended and noted that a Negro served the pastor at the communion service; she decided to join because of the witness of brotherhood.

When those of Japanese ancestry were being relocated during the war, Mt. Hollywood members served them coffee and sandwiches as they gathered at buses to go to the unknown. Later, the pastor visited many of them at the centers, and members cared for the Japanese church building. In appreciation, the nisei gave Mt. Hollywood a gift of money when they returned.

After long discussion, the congregation decided to spend the money for a cross from atom-bombed Japan. The symbol was made from the charred and once radioactive wood of the camphor tree in the atom-blasted Hiroshima church garden of the Rev. K. Tanimoto, Methodist pastor who was one of the characters in John Hersey's *Hiroshima*. A member of the church brought the wood to the United States, and Mr. Tanimoto spoke at Mt. Hollywood when the cross was installed.

"It was perhaps the most important meeting we have ever had in our church," Mr. Hunter observes.

In a working class neighborhood of Pasadena, California, the Lincoln Avenue Methodist church integrated instead of moving. Today it is interracial, with 15 per cent Negro membership. An assistant minister and the head of its women's society are Negroes.

In Los Angeles, the Disciples' McCarty Memorial Church decided to stay put when the neighborhood became racially mixed and seven other churches on its avenue moved. Now it has a growing, aggressive congregation of 437. In 1954-55, eighty-seven new members—twenty-nine of them Negro—were received. Japanese and Chinese also belong to this church.

"It is bringing a real spiritual rebirth to our people," says the Rev. Kring Allen.

A long-integrated Disciples congregation is at First Church in Pittsburg, Kansas. The open policy began thirty years ago, and the church now includes eight Negro and seventeen Spanish-American members.

Many integrated churches are in big cities, but a remarkable exception is Bethel Methodist Church, which is surrounded by farms and strip mines in the Steubenville district of eastern Ohio. About 1945, members were considering closing its doors. Then its vitality picked up, and one reason was Negro attendance. In 1940, after a Negro janitor was hired, a few Negroes had begun to attend. Not until 1954, however, did the first Negro join. Often as many as twenty-two Negroes attend this little church whose total membership is seventy-nine.

"The church is in the best condition spiritually it has been my experience to know," reports the Rev. Charles F. Rothel.

¶Integration in the Southern Churches

The growth of interracial churches in the South is perhaps an even more dramatic story. While many Northern churches debate whether to accept Negroes, several Southern congregations have been giving a positive answer.

One of the most inspiring stories of Christian fellowship that ignores racial lines is that of a Methodist church in Norman, Oklahoma. This church has grown interracially as if that were the most natural thing in the world, according to its pastor. None of the incidents reported from some Northern congregations have marred this development.

The church is the McFarlin Memorial Methodist, with more than three thousand members and a constituency that regularly numbers in excess of 4,500, since the congregation includes many students at the University of Oklahoma. Nine out of ten members have a long Southern heritage. Oklahoma has typical Southern Jim Crow laws, but "these do not deter us," says the minister, the Rev. Finis A. Crutchfield Jr.

"We have never been a segregated church," Mr. Crutchfield declares. "We did not have to desegregate our church. It was, I suppose, desegregated from the beginning. Not wishing to be misunderstood, our Board of Stewards on one occasion did adopt a resolution explaining that any child of God could worship and fully participate in the life of this church. The resolution was not specifically directed toward any race group but toward any person on earth."

In fact, the minister says, he doubts that Negroes are denied membership in any Methodist church of the state. There are many, many Oklahoma churches in which no Negroes are members, he adds, but no Methodist church is actually segregated.

"There are a number of Negroes who participate fully in the life and fellowship of our congregation," reports Mr. Crutchfield. "They belong, they take up the offering, they take their turn ushering, they participate in the social life of the congregation, and we are not cognizant at all of their darker skin. We also have a number of Indians in this congregation; of course, this is not uncommon at all."

But doesn't this cause trouble?

"Not a single objection has been experienced from any quarter whatsoever that I consider significant," replies the minister. "Not one single person has left the church or its membership because of the presence of Negroes. As a matter of fact, we take it as a matter of course. I think this would be true of the majority of Oklahoma Methodists."

Mr. Crutchfield is himself a Southerner. Born and reared in Texas, he was educated in North Carolina. He believes on the one hand that extremist positions never solve anything, but on the other that compromising positions are not Christian.

In the last three years, a white minister in Galveston, Texas, has succeeded in creating an interracial church. Immediately after his graduation from General Theological Seminary, New York, in 1953, the Rev. Fred W. Sutton Jr., took over an all-Negro Episcopal congregation in the Texas church. A number of white members have joined.

About 1950, the Woodlawn Christian Church in San Antonio received its first non-Caucasian members. It now includes two Negro and four Mexican-American members.

First Unitarian Church of Houston has accepted a Negro family since a 104 to 12 vote of the congregation in 1954 approved an open policy. Three Negro children are in the church school. "Negroes have attended our socials, and insofar as it is possible, tension being as it is in the South, we believe we are on the road to an integrated church," writes the Rev. Horace F. Westwood, pastor.

As Washington, D. C. is a focus of interest about secular handling of the race problem, so is it for the church. In 1955, Calvary Baptist Church there voted to admit Miss Florence Davis, a student from Liberia. Though colored foreigners are sometimes interracially placed in a more fa-

vorable category than American Negroes, she was considered
as Negro in the debate; so the vote of 129 to 79 for her
admittance made this the first white Baptist church in the
capital to take in a Negro member. Later, Calvary agreed to
accept GI's, Negro as well as white, recommended by Baptist
chaplains.

Advocates argued that rejection of Miss Davis, a graduate of mission schools, would hurt the mission cause. It
would be a repudiation of Christ's teachings and give the
Communists propaganda ammunition. The minority contended "God put different races in the world and they
should stay that way."

According to a Washington paper, about forty Negroes
belong to ten predominantly white Protestant churches in
the capital. The denominations include Disciples, Lutheran,
Protestant Episcopal, Unitarian, Friends, Congregational,
and Church of the Savior (ecumenical).

The Associated Press reported that five large Protestant
churches in Atlanta, Georgia, have agreed quietly to accept
Negro applicants. "Even the diehards down here recognize
that it is only a matter of time," the Christian Council secretary told the Associated Press.

One of the most inspiring stories of a Christian fellowship across racial lines is that of a church in North Carolina.
The Baptist Church in Brookford, an all-white textile town,
has been integrated for about eighteen years. This unusual
interracial experiment came about because the white pastor
was shaken by a sudden insight that he should try it.

The Rev. W. C. Laney is a stout, balding man who was
born in a log cabin in Lincoln County in 1894. As a boy

he was a mill hand and got no formal education. At twenty-four he began to work his way through college.

After his sudden change of heart in 1938, he invited Negroes to join his church. His white congregation backed him up, though some whites in the community still grumble about his long-time pioneering. There have been as many as twenty-five Negro members, but only about five now regularly attend, in a congregation of 120. Mrs. Bessie Wells, a lively young Negro trained in New York, leads the twenty-six-voice choir, which includes two Negro girls.

Some teen-age Negro girls who attend usually arrive on Saturday night, eat with the white members, and stay overnight in an addition to the church. Like whites, they have to refute the intermarriage bugaboo. Geraldine Cline, a seventeen-year-old from Shelby, for example, explains that her parents objected: "The first thing they said at home was that a white boy will fall in love with me or I will fall in love with a white boy. They say it is a terrible sin to marry a white boy. But you don't join up with a white church to marry. I find something here I don't find in my own church. It makes me feel like a real person. For the first time I feel like a real person."

Mr. Laney tells how his change came at a Baptist ministers' meeting where segregation was discussed. He began to ponder his own outlook, and God spoke.

"I was so prejudiced that I refused to shake a Negro's hand before I heard God speak to me," he recalls. "Suddenly a whole new world opened to me. . . . I went out of the tiny world into the great world of God that moment."

6 HOW HIGH DOES
EQUALITY GO?

S THE CHURCHES GIVE UP SEGREGA-
tion in attendance and membership, the question naturally arises: Should Negroes have
equal rights to serve as leaders in the church?

The Christian must make the same choice
as the businessman who has decided to hire
Negroes as assembly line workers and then
wonders whether he should upgrade the best
to supervisory positions. Though the moral answer may be clear, practical agreement on such
questions is not. The church has had women as
members from the first, for example, but you
can still get a good debate going on whether
women should become ministers!

There are many signs that Protestants are
becoming more willing to give members of mi-

nority groups an equal chance for posts where they can lead. In St. Paul, Minnesota, in 1955, for example, some of the members of the state Methodist conference decided it would be a good idea to elect a certain qualified member, a Negro, as a ministerial delegate to the General Conference. In order to make this possible, two ministers high in the running withdrew, threw their support behind Charles M. Sexton, pastor of a church in a Negro section of Minneapolis, and he won.

Mr. Sexton, having spent a summer on an evangelistic mission in Japan, commented that the action would help show the Orient that Christian democracy really works in this country.

Similarly, in Toledo, Ohio, leaders of the Council of Churches elected a Negro president for the first time. The choice was the Rev. Joseph Smith, pastor of St. Paul's Baptist Church for twenty-seven years.

The Rev. Benjamin F. Glasco was installed as moderator of the Philadelphia Presbytery in 1954. He was the first Negro to be elected to this high office in the presbytery, the largest in the Presbyterian Church in the U. S. A.

Interracial leadership at the top levels was noteworthy at the assembly of the World Council of Churches in Evanston in 1954. Speakers represented many races; one of the most popular was Benjamin E. Mays, an American Negro and president of Morehouse College, Atlanta.

A cynic might object that this was all show, that the American church delegations were lily-white; but he would be wrong. For example, the Rev. Clarence T. R. Nelson, part-time representative of Methodist Information, a Negro doing church journalistic work, pointed out that Negro

Methodists had a significant place at Evanston. Four of the denomination's thirty-six official delegates were Negroes, he said; so were six of the fifty-four Methodist accredited visitors. Among the seventeen Methodists serving as consultants, one was a Negro.

Other Negro delegates at Evanston included Rosa Page Welch, a well-known Negro singer, of the Disciples, and Dr. Shelby Rooks, of St. James Presbyterian Church, New York (whose wife, Dorothy Maynor, is another famous singer).

Negro churchmen were honored in two 1956 events at the top level of Protestantism: Bishop D. Ward Nichols of the African Methodist Episcopal Church served on the nine-man National Council deputation to Russia. J. Ernest Wilkins, assistant secretary of labor, became first Negro head of Methodism's powerful Judicial Council.

Negroes are becoming ministers in both "white" and unsegregated churches, and they are being sent as missionaries.

Mission boards were long slow about sending Negroes to other parts of the world than Africa. But was the white man—this representative of the "imperialist" race—the best person to take the Christian message to colored peoples? Under the impact of such questions, boards have been changing their policies.

The first Negro missionary I ever met was in Turkey. The Congregationalists had sent Bob King, an Ohio Methodist, former football star and New York City boys' worker, out to teach. It was fitting that he was in Tarsus, home town of a most famous missionary. Bob, who was teaching biology, chemistry, and athletics, said he was the denomination's

first Negro missionary to a non-African field. The dusky
Turkish boys welcomed him without a hint of color feeling.

Later, in India, I found another American Negro at work.
He was Lawrence Burr of Chicago, whom the YMCA had
sent to serve as a Y leader in the southern Indian city of
Madras. In a slum area, Burr was running a recreation
center for skinny little boys who made a precarious living
on the city streets; homeless, some of them slept on the
walks.

A young man from St. Louis, Myron Ross, finished Eden
Seminary in 1953 and became the first Negro minister in
the Evangelical and Reformed Church. For a time, he was
pastor of a community church in Overland, Missouri. Recently he was named a missionary to Japan.

In the home field of this denomination, Lela Mae Satoe,
a Kiowa Indian girl from Oklahoma, has been serving as
a children's worker at the Denver Christian Center. Under
her leadership, these youngsters naturally learn about other
races and peoples, and though they themselves have few
possessions, they contributed $6.37 for children in Alaska.

In late 1955, the Rev. Charles E. Boddie was named associate secretary in the Department of Missionary Personnel,
the American Baptist Foreign Mission Societies—the first
Negro to get an executive post with the group. At the same
time, the Baptists appointed the first Negro foreign missionaries in several years—Mr. and Mrs. Milton A. Combs, who
were assigned to Burma.

In "a new departure, although not a new policy," the
Baptists have also assigned an Oriental girl to the Orient.
Estelle Miao Schock is the daughter of the Rev. Chester

Miao, a Chinese Christian active in world church affairs and still a church leader in Red China. She came to America to study, received her master's degree from Berkeley Baptist Divinity School, and married Harold Schock. The Schocks served as home missionaries to the American Indians in Nevada and then were sent to work in Rangoon, Burma.

About fifty Negro missionaries and a scattered handful of missionaries of Asian ancestry have been sent overseas by U. S. churches, according to a bulletin of the Missionary Research Library. At most, there are two hundred nonwhite missionaries among the nineteen thousand serving United States and Canadian boards. This leaves a long way to go to real equality. However, heads of fifty-seven of these boards say they will accept qualified applicants of all races.

The Baptists also get credit for another interesting venture in church work at home. In 1951, the Rev. Henry Mitchell, a Negro home missionary on the West Coast, was given the position of missionary extension and building representative of the Northern California convention. In addition to responsibility for Negro churches, he now handles real estate, loans, and organization for a vastly expanded program.

Some say that he is successful because he doesn't look like a Negro. With medium tan skin, straight dark hair, and a narrow mustache, Mr. Mitchell might be taken for a Latin. But he doubts that this makes any difference, partly because he was known for six years as a Negro missionary in the same area.

"While I may not look like a Negro, my wife and children do," he says. "My wife has had a happy experience in her nation-wide labors as an American Baptist instructor of church school teachers."

Born in South Carolina, Mrs. Mitchell has a master's degree from Union Theological Seminary, New York, where her husband also was graduated. She is now a children's worker for the First Baptist Church in Oakland, the first person of color on the staff of this white church. She also teaches at a Baptist divinity school.

Mr. Mitchell recalls that he got his present administrative job, not as a racial experiment, but as a move toward staff efficiency. Anxious to prove himself, he realized suddenly that he was fearful. Before long he faced an especially tough task for a Negro: getting a change in some restrictive property covenants. It was necessary to persuade four couples who owned lots to agree to let them be used as the site of a church rather than holding them for the erection of private homes. Mr. Mitchell had architects' plans showing that the church building would fit into the neighborhood nicely. Yet he was fearful about trying to "sell" the project.

He began by meeting with three men from the church. They prayed together in a car and then started.

"We went forth two by two to get signatures," he explains. "On these depended a title policy, and on this depended the building loan for a New Frontiers church. Not a single family refused us. What a cause for rejoicing!"

One thing he learned that day was that the issue was not race, that Christians should assume in such cases that color is immaterial. Another thing he learned was that Southerners—many Baptists in his section come from the South—are friendly.

"Time and again I have found people from 'down yon-dah' hospitably insisting that I save missionary money by eating and sleeping in their homes," he declares. "A most safe and conservative judgment would be that Southern ex-traction has not at any place been a liability to brotherhood in my work."

One of his biggest satisfactions has been feeling that in a lifetime of seeming rebuffs God was preparing him for this special job.

"I have the feeling also that God must have prepared others —others whom we may have overlooked. Next time you ask God for a kingdom servant, ask him to look among *all* his children."

¶*Equal Rights in the Pulpit*

"But," objects someone, "I might approve of a Negro do-ing missionary work somewhere—but do you think people would want someone of a different race right in their own pulpit?"

"Yes," reply many Protestants.

For example, in a poll at the Community Methodist Church in San Bruno, California, twenty-five members said they would find a nonwhite minister acceptable; three had no opinion, and seven said he would be unacceptable. Such an overwhelming majority is probably not surprising when one considers that the congregation already includes Filipino and Negro couples.

This suggests that—outside the Negro churches, of course —an integrated congregation may be the most likely to suc-ceed with a Negro ministry. This is the kind of church, for instance, in which a Negro pastor has accepted a pastorate in Detroit.

John T. Walker, though young, has been a race-relations pioneer for some years. A graduate of Wayne University, he became the first Negro to attend Virginia Theological Seminary, and while still a student began work in St. Mary's Episcopal Church in Detroit.

This congregation is 80 per cent white and 20 per cent Negro. When Negroes began to move into the neighborhood, members of the church decided to open its doors and, not without soul searching, they achieved integration successfully. Attendance went up. Contributions increased. And Mr. Walker, at twenty-nine, was chosen rector. He is said to be the first man of his race to become minister of a predominantly white Episcopal congregation.

Another Middlewestern church, an all-white one, has called a minister who is unique in two respects—the new pastor is a Negro and a woman. Mrs. Ozie G. Wattleton, who was doing home mission work for the Church of God in Mississippi, hesitated to go to the congregation of this denomination in Columbus, a Nebraska town of ten thousand. What would be the reaction to herself, her husband, and their daughter? Could Alyce Faye go to school?

Church members had heard her give a good talk at a national gathering and asked her to speak at a series of Nebraska meetings. When she did, the congregation was sure she should be called. She decided to accept.

The arrangement worked beautifully. The family was well received. The church program expanded. New families joined. One member, asked whether he was embarrassed about having a Negro pastor, replied: "Oh, is she colored? We really hadn't noticed."

The Congregational Christian churches in Connecticut have for some time had at least two nonwhite ministers— James B. Yee, (a Chinese) at East Hampton, and Roland T. Heacock, at Staffordsville. Mr. Heacock says: "The past five years have been filled with warm and cordial pastor-and-people relationship, unmarred by any blighting racial incident. My members are all white. I am a Negro."

Dr. Jitsuo Morikawa, formerly pastor of the First Baptist Church in Chicago and now director of evangelism of the American Baptist Convention, is a Japanese-American, up-rooted from the West Coast during World War II. When relocated Japanese settled near the church, Dr. Morikawa was first called to be co-pastor. Later he became full pastor, a position he held for a decade. He was one of the American Baptist delegates to the World Council meetings in Evanston.

Another "first" of this decade was the installation of the first Negro to become pastor of a Reformed Church in America. The Rev. James Joshua Thomas, son of a Presbyterian minister, was educated at Lincoln University in Pennsylvania and at Drew Theological Seminary, Madison, New Jersey. After serving as a Presbyterian pastor in the British West Indies, he came to study at Columbia University in New York City and assisted on the staff of First Reformed Church in Astoria, Queens.

The Mott Haven Reformed Church, a predominantly white congregation in the midst of a Bronx neighborhood where most of the residents are nonwhite, decided to integrate and named Mr. Thomas the stated supply pastor for twelve months. The result was a sharp revival. Attendance at Sunday school went as high as 268, with 75 per cent of the children Negro.

In late 1954, Mr. Thomas, at thirty-five, was installed as regular pastor. He was the first of his race in the 325 years of this one-time Dutch church, significantly a sister church of the South African Reformed Church that supports *apartheid*. But at his installation, segregation was not even mentioned.

"We are all together, participating in a great experience," the presiding minister, Dr. Ernest R. Palen, said afterward.

Other recent appointments of Negro pastors to white congregations include the Rev. A. L. Reynolds Jr., of Topeka, Kansas, to Sixth United Presbyterian Church on Chicago's South Side, and the Rev. Joseph R. Washington Jr., of Woburn, Massachusetts, to lead two Maine churches, one Congregational and the other Methodist.

The Rev. Robert T. Neilssen, twenty-eight-year-old white Lutheran, recently became pastor of a large Negro Lutheran church in Harlem. In Columbia, South Carolina, Dr. R. E. Huffman, forty-three-year-old white physician, applied to the African Methodist Episcopal Church for recognition as a minister.

Meantime, a South Carolina Negro, a Methodist, made interracial news in New England.

Simon Peter Montgomery was born in 1922, son of a poor Southern farmer. At fourteen, he went to work for a dollar a day in a lumber yard in Pineville, South Carolina. That was when his father died and he had to quit school to support his mother. Later, he got back to school, put himself through seminary, and was ordained an elder in 1947. He served churches in Rock Hill and Gaffney.

He went North, and from 1952 to 1954 did graduate work at Garrett Biblical Institute and preached at a Negro church in Evanston. He then went East to study at Boston University. In Massachusetts he came to the attention of Bishop John Wesley Lord of the Boston area, who soon appointed him director of Christian education at the oldest and largest Methodist church in Maine.

But the big news about Mr. Montgomery came after he had won his master's degree in the spring of 1955. The pastor of the venerable Methodist Church at Old Mystic, Connecticut, had resigned. Would a Negro be a suitable replacement?

Mr. Montgomery's name was proposed, and the congregation heard him preach two Sundays. The Rev. Charles X. Hutchinson Jr., the district superintendent, strongly recommended him. Bishop Lord was ready and eager to make the appointment. How about it? The local selection committee met and discussed Mr. Montgomery, and the question of his race did not even come up! He was agreed on.

"We just wanted a good pastor," explained Roland Avery, board chairman. "Mr. Montgomery is a good speaker. He picks out a Bible topic and discusses it from every viewpoint. He really explains it, and he doesn't raise his voice."

"I think it's wonderful," said Mrs. Charles Metzermacher, superintendent of the church school. A woman who has been a member for fifty years, summed up for all: "He is smart, sincere, and capable. What difference does his color make?"

After his inaugural service, the new thirty-three-year-old pastor stood in his dark robes on the steps of the neat white clapboard church, shook hands with the members, and told them: "This church has planted a seed that will sprout brotherly love throughout the world."

Methodists, searching their memories, decided that history had been written at Old Mystic. Negroes have served mixed Methodist congregations. They have served white congregations temporarily. But this was the first time a Negro had become regular minister for a white Methodist church.

To Old Mystic came a telegram of congratulations from the Rev. Ralph T. Templin, the first white minister to join a Negro Methodist conference and Wesley foundation director at a Negro college in Wilberforce, Ohio: "Your appointment is Methodism's success. Pray our approaches from two sides of the same problem may meet in God's time in one world family of Wesley's parish."

That was the hope of a good many American Protestants for their denominations as they pondered race and the ministry.

¶Ministers in Crisis

If some churches have begun to bring equality, others have made their leaders suffer for advocating it. Several white ministers and religious educators have been fired because their views on race seemed too advanced.

The rural Baptist congregation at Lumpkin, Georgia, asked for the resignation of the Rev. Robert Trotman after he praised the court decision on schools as just and Christian. The story of the resignation of another Baptist pastor, the Rev. Henry A. Buchanan, at Shellman, Georgia, was told in Chapter 4. In South Carolina, the Rev. George Jackson Stafford, a Baptist leader in the state, resigned from the governor's home-town church after what was called an "informal dispute" about integration.

At the Fortune Baptist Church near Parkin, Arkansas, the Rev. E. Jones preached on church segregation in 1954. He was warned not to do it again. In 1955 he preached condemning segregation in church as unchristian, and was dismissed by a forty-three to seven vote.

The Rev. Marsh Callaway, Presbyterian pastor in Durant, Mississippi, criticized a segregationist mass meeting as "unchristian and un-American." He was asked to resign. Another Mississippi pastor, the Rev. Roy C. Delamotte, also lost his pulpit on the segregation issue.

At the University of Florida, the Rev. W. Thaxton Springfield, Methodist student pastor, urged that Negro students be admitted. Asking him to quit, the local Wesley Foundation Board expressed fear that he would "confuse our young people." Miss Jolee Fritz, director of the Wesley Foundation at Greensboro, North Carolina, was also asked to resign because of her liberal race views and membership in the NAACP.

Late in 1955, noting that "at least five ministers" had already been forced to resign on the race issue, the National Council of Churches asked the denominations to find new posts for them.

Martyrdom for their views has come also to Negro ministers. In Belzoni, Mississippi, the Rev. George W. Lee was the first of his race to register to vote in his county. He was warned in the spring of 1955 to remove his name, but he refused. One night a car overtook him on a dark street, and two gangster-style blasts from a shotgun killed him. There have been no arrests.

A few months later, the African Methodist Episcopal Church of the Rev. Joseph A. DeLaine, pastor in Lake City, South Carolina, who advocated school integration, was burned down. Four days later, eight cars surrounded his home. Segregationists fired at his family and he fired back. The family fled. When they got to New York, an unsuccessful effort was made to extradite him as a fugitive from justice.

Negro ministers have been the leaders in the recent resistance against segregation in the South. Montgomery, Alabama, the one-time capital of the Confederacy, in 1956 became the symbol of the struggle; but as early as August, 1955, Negroes had begun a boycott of twenty-three Orangeburg, South Carolina, merchants who had joined the White Citizens Council. The group was led by three Negro ministers—Methodist, Baptist, and Episcopal—and a Roman Catholic priest. When the whites met with the Negroes to seek a settlement in the spring of 1956, it constituted the first successful non-violent resistance in the South of today.

In Montgomery in December, 1955, a Negro woman refused to give her seat to a white man on a bus, and another protest began. Though forty thousand Negroes had been riding these buses, 99 per cent started a boycott that lasted for months. Car pools were organized, and a Montgomery Improvement Association was established, with the Rev. Martin Luther King Jr., son and grandson of ministers, as president. This quiet young Negro, who is the minister of a Negro Baptist church, has lived all his life in the South except for a brief period of study in northern schools. Significantly, mass meetings in the Negro churches became the heart of the resistance movement, and twenty-six ministers and many civic leaders were indicted for participation. As this is written, their cases are still in the courts.

Around the nation, churches at all levels expressed their support for the movement. Some had all-night prayer vigils. In Montgomery, the ministerial association urged citizens to "lay aside passion" and seek "an agreeable solution." Seventeen Negro ministers met and prayed together. Among the white ministers, the Rev. Thomas Thrasher, an Episcopalian, has spoken quietly against extremism and for moderation. The only white man to join five thousand Negroes in the original protest was the Rev. Robert S. Graetz, the young pastor of an "almost all-Negro" Lutheran mission congregation. When he helped drive in the car pool, Mr. Graetz was arrested and lectured on how the Bible supports segregation.

"They can't figure you out, Bob," the city editor of a Montgomery daily told him, "because you're a Christian."

The most dramatic highlight of the protest came when the home of Dr. King was bombed while he was at a meeting. He rushed to the house, found his wife and small daughter safe. Then he addressed the hundreds who were milling around the place. "Do not hate, do not become violent," he said, "but love!"

Gandhi-like, Dr. King's message is that violence is impractical and immoral. The Montgomery resistance, he explains, rests on spiritual forces: "Love *must* be at the forefront of our movement if it is to be a successful movement. And when we speak of love, we speak of understanding, good will toward *all* men. We speak of a creative, a redemptive sort of love. . . . Someone must have sense enough and morality enough to cut off the chain of hate and evil. The greatest way to do that is through love."

7   OF ROOTS AND BRANCHES

NNA BELLE HOOTON, A PRETTY TEEN-
ager with bright eyes and a gamin hairdo, was
active in the Methodist Youth Fellowship at
Mount Vernon Place Church and a senior in
Eastern High School. The time: the fall when
Southern schools were first facing integration
under the Supreme Court's dictum. The place:
Washington, D. C.

In nearby Delaware and Maryland, students
had been striking. Now rumors came that they
were going to walk out also at Eastern, where
nine hundred Negro students were being integrated with about one thousand white. Why
not let them strike? Ann felt she had a special obligation to avoid that, for she had been
elected president of the student council as a

representative of all the boys and girls enrolled—and she was a Christian.

"We ought to respect people for the abilities they have, not for their color," she explained later. "The reason I believe this is that I was brought up in a Christian family. The problem is to promote equal rights for all, and I should think any Christian would be in favor of that."

She went first to the principal, and he called an assembly. When the students came in, they found their own council on the stage. The principal and Ann both spoke briefly.

"Do you think a strike will really accomplish anything?" she asked. "Why don't we do something that is more likely to settle things?"

But unpersuaded, eight hundred white pupils didn't show up next morning. That left only two hundred of them—including Ann and the other council members—going to class. Her friends tried to get her to stop attending. Some of her "best friends" even stopped speaking to her.

Ann and the others continued to go, however, and slowly the strike lost its strength. Soon most of the students were back in class. How could Christian reconciliation be brought in this tense atmosphere of surly dislike?

Someone said that New Rochelle, New York, had a good interracial program, and Ann and five other students from troubled schools went to observe the New Rochelle classes. When they got back, she suggested that Eastern High form an interracial citizenship council to discuss social problems as they came up.

Perfection has not come to Eastern as a quick result, of

course, but because one Christian girl tried to act on her beliefs, the forces of division, hate, and just plain indifference were rolled back on one little sector. Later, Anna Belle Hooton had this simple word for other young people: "Stand up for what you believe!"

¶Youth and Women Show the Way

The story of Ann Hooton is one of many illustrating the way young people lead in improving attitudes on race. Oldsters bequeath to them institutions that contain fossilized lines of separation; yet given a chance, youth often wipes out the divisions. Instance after instance can be cited:

In Philadelphia, some young people at a Negro church heard a talk by a Honduran girl who had received a scholarship from Evangelical and Reformed youth; impressed, they invited some white young people from an Evangelical and Reformed church over to get acquainted.

In Colorado, a United Christian Youth Mission was set up on an interracial basis.

In Maryland, a Methodist senior high institute voted 222 to two to give up the usual swimming program because a private pool would not admit Negro delegates with the rest. A Southern Methodist student conference that included nine Negro delegates, meeting in North Carolina, similarly boycotted segregated swimming.

In Ohio, national youth leaders voted to try to include more Negro colleges in the Student Christian Movement.

In Texas, Cindy Bowser of Dallas, who was in a church group that had attended an interracial youth meeting in

Arkansas the week before, proposed a resolution to a Methodist youth assembly. Without an opposing voice, the Texas young people voted that they would take an active part in the leadership toward the abolishment of segregation and would cooperate fully with others trying to follow Christ in this Christian endeavor.

Each year since 1948, a group of Northern young people has visited Nashville, Tennessee, to study and experience better race relations. They are members of the Stanley Congregational Church of Chatham, New Jersey, where their experience in race relations has been confined to contacts with Negro servants.

Church editors for Protestant young people have also led in educating for better race relations. For example, *Youth,* the Evangelical and Reformed magazine, rarely fails to have something on intercultural relations. It has published a "comic" strip about Booker T. Washington, Anti-Defamation League cartoons, and articles about the Harlem Globe Trotters and a Negro member of the Los Angeles Rams football team, who was becoming a minister.

The youth work camp is one of the church's newer institutions that is almost invariably interracial. Several denominations have for years had such camps where teenagers work and worship together, perhaps painting the walls of a tenement room, maybe remodeling a store as a chapel.

In the last decade, the work camp idea has been taken up by the World Council of Churches, with enthusiastic backing from American youth. Ecumenical camps, held now in Europe and Asia as well as America, go far in being "inter" —international, interdenominational, interracial.

A Quaker-led organization, the American Friends Service Committee, is the outstanding pioneer of the work camp. Though a book could be written about AFSC camps alone, we will simply note that they have been sponsored not only in this country but in such distant nations as Poland and Finland. For fifteen and more years, several thousand young workers have helped in week-end camps in the Quaker city, Philadelphia.

One group of Methodist work-campers found out how really pioneering they were when they tried to do some painting at a church school in Camden, South Carolina, in the summer of 1956. Ten whites and five Negroes tried to work together, but segregationists telephoned threats and burned a cross in front of the school. The campers decided they had better move out. They were welcomed into another interracial Methodist camp at Olive Hill, in the mountains of eastern Kentucky. The Presbyterians have had an interracial work camp at an academy in Georgia.

The work of the Evangelical and Reformed Church in St. Louis is a good example of the way the summer work camp helps young people to better race attitudes through work with different groups. Years ago, in one of the slum areas of the city, a woman contributed fifty cents to a group of seminary boys to get them to do some Christian work there. As a result, they started a Sunday school class with five boys. That was the simple beginning in 1913 of the Caroline Mission, which today has a dozen staff workers.

For decades, the work was all white, though the neighborhood was mixed. But in 1943, with assistance from a laundry owner and from the American Friends Service

Committee, the mission started an interracial playground. Some of the youngsters asked whether they could attend vacation church school; they were Negroes, so the mission decided it should "open up."

There was a chance to start a camp. Should it be segregated? The leaders, deciding against segregation, named it Camp TAMBO, from the Scripture, "that all may be one." Then the mission social clubs also opened up; six now have both Negro and white members. A Negro scout whose scoutmaster was drafted asked some fellow campers about joining the all-white troop, and the Scouts, too, opened up.

How has it worked out?

There was the teen-age troublemaker who later won a sportsmanship award on an interracial mission ball team. There was a Negro girl, rejected by the white church, and rejecting it in turn, who gradually decided to enter a life of Christian service. Little successes, but very important ones.

In 1943, the Evangelical and Reformed Church decided to start a Fellowship Center in another St. Louis area filled with dilapidated houses, dark hallways, rats, and crowded rooms. An old tavern was converted, and settlement and camp work began. The Disciples now cooperate by providing an associate pastor.

The center serves the neighborhood without regard to race, nationality, or religion, and the church there has a large sprinkling of Negroes. In putting up a new center building recently, the leaders engraved on the cornerstone a verse from the Psalms: "Behold how good and how pleasant it is for the brethren to dwell together in unity."

To both this mission and this center in St. Louis, young people of the church have come to give typical work camp aid. One team of ten caravanners, for example, worked with the staff members, shared devotions, bought groceries, prepared meals, and did laundry. They also helped on the playgrounds, taught Bible school, and acted as counsellors in the camps. Afterwards, one of the college girls told how her Christian responsibility to love all human beings had been jarred awake by her experiences in working at the interracial camp.

"There were five Negro girls and two white girls in my cabin," she explained, "but no prejudice problems existed. One night I tucked the girls into bed and they asked me to kiss them all good night. The lights were out. Not until then did I realize I couldn't see the color. And since they had switched the beds, there was no difference."

Like the youngsters, the women of the Protestant churches have been active in making their fellowships interracial. United Church Women has been pressing local councils of church women to take forward steps in connection with this concern, from wherever they are, under a directive that was enacted at Omaha in 1952.

Leaders have urged that women's meetings, at all levels, be checked to see whether there is good racial representation in attendance, planning, and program participation. They have asked also that boards, committees, officers' slates, and delegations be examined for inclusiveness, and have proposed to individual women a pledge to make everyday actions show "belief that all persons are children of God."

¶Color, Councils, and Conferences

One way in which churches try to break with discriminatory social patterns is in demanding that those housing their conferences treat all delegates alike. When the Massachusetts Baptist Convention planned its 1955 fall meeting in a hotel at Haverhill, the reservation of one speaker, a Negro professor from Drew University, was rejected. The convention promptly arranged to house all its speakers in the homes of churchmen instead. In this instance, the hotel owner quickly apologized and offered to take all delegates—regardless of color and in spite of what other guests might feel.

A widely publicized clash on housing a church meeting was that which involved plans to hold the 1955 Protestant Episcopal triennial in Houston, Texas. Bishop Clinton S. Quin of Texas arranged for nonsegregated meals and a nonsegregated motel, but Negro delegates would still have been barred from hotels and restaurants and forced to use separate rest rooms. Diocesan conventions in New York and Washington protested. Presiding Bishop Henry Knox Sherrill decided to cancel the meeting in Houston and move the triennial to Honolulu.

"I am certain," said the Bishop, "that the witness of our church must be so clear that it need not be explained."

The Houston incident may have created a wrong impression of Texas, however, for actually that state has recently taken many steps to break down the color line.

Presbyterians in Texas and Oklahoma have been integrating their synods. In Austin, two Negro churches were admitted to the Austin Baptist Association—first in the history of the Southern Baptist Convention. Dr. Ed Bratcher of Austin, born and reared on the mission field, said: "It is difficult for a missionary in Africa to explain why his converts cannot attend Southern Baptist churches."

Meantime, Dallas, Texas, has been holding interracial concerts. The choirs of four Methodist churches, two African Methodist Episcopal churches, and a high school chorus joined under Bandleader Fred Waring in one of these, heard by 4,200.

One reason for the push toward integration is that the Christian good news is not for a select few, but for all. Obviously, the logical pressure for treating everyone alike is at its highest in evangelism efforts. It is no accident that institutions for evangelizing are beginning to ignore color.

Both North and South have had interracial preaching missions. An outstanding example was the United Preaching Mission at Norfolk, Virginia, in 1955. This was the first time it was held on an interracial basis, and the step was taken purposely by its sponsors, the Norfolk Ministers Association, which is now interracial. Ten denominations and more than one hundred churches were represented by the two score nationally-known speakers, including two Negroes. *The Norfolk Ledger-Dispatch* said: "It marks an advanced step in an interracial movement which has been gaining strength in this community in recent years."

The Rev. Charles B. Templeton, well-known evangelist, has had some success in demanding that all races be admitted to his missions. The problem is not only in the South, he believes. Segregation is less clearly defined but just as real in the North. The church is not providing the vigorous sacrificial leadership that is necessary, he says, and too few churches "are making anything other than passive efforts to break down racial barriers."

In the South, declares Mr. Templeton, the ministers, while sometimes timid, are eager to do all they can to erase the lines. "It is possible, by insisting upon it, to get cities on the northern edge of the South to acquiesce to the demand that audiences be unsegregated. In the Deep South this is nearly impossible."

Nevertheless, he has held missions with unsegregated audiences below the Mason-Dixon Line, without serious incident. "This situation is rapidly improving," he summarizes, "but it is yet far from ideal."

Evangelist Billy Graham says he tries to set an example and permits no segregation at his meetings. He has had integrated gatherings in New Orleans, Nashville, Richmond, and Oklahoma City, and had "no problem at all."

Indicative of the transition under way is the action of the Raleigh, North Carolina, Ministerial Association. It recently established a policy requiring that all its future community ecumenical services be interracial.

One quiet, almost unnoticed shift is the change in ministerial associations. Southern ministers' groups such as those in Norfolk and Raleigh have been widening their fellowships. In St. Petersburg and Bradenton, Florida, the associations voted to admit Negro pastors to full membership.

As 1955 ended, the *Christian Advocate* reported a survey which showed that during the preceding eighteen months "more than a dozen groups" of ministers had be-

come interracial; and several other cities in the South re-
ported they were working for the change. There are, ac-
cording to the *Advocate,* new interracial associations in
Nashville, Baltimore, Louisville, Daytona Beach, and four
North Carolina cities—Asheville, Salisbury, Greensboro, and
High Point.

In Selma, Alabama, where one of the interracial associations was organized, the Rev. Lemuel B. Green said its
spirit had been "fine." Some Negro pastors were suspicious
about joining, but there has been no community opposition.

"Leadership is equally shared," declared Mr. Green. "For
the next few years we are agreed that the president be a
white man in order to facilitate contacts with officialdom
until we are established. The vice-president and treasurer
are Negroes."

How important a ministerial association with good attitudes can be was illustrated at Lakewood, a suburb of
Cleveland, Ohio. Except for Negro custodians and servants,
it is an all-white community. Without warning, someone
heaved a seventeen pound rock through the window of an
apartment occupied by one custodian, his wife, and their
twelve-year-old daughter. Anonymous phone threats followed. Why? Apparently because the girl had gotten her
picture in the papers for winning a marble tournament.

Lakewood ministers went to work. A committee of their
association reassured the family and issued an appeal "to
give these people a fair chance to make their way in our
land of equality and of Christian brotherhood." Others
joined the clergymen, and the family stayed in Lakewood.

Meantime, in Cleveland itself, vandals hurled acid at

newly painted homes of young Negroes who had moved into a white area. Newspapers, labor, and business issued protests. The ministerial associations passed resolutions, but four Cleveland ministers decided to go further. Led by John Wilkes, a Baptist pastor, they took paint and brushes and painted two of the acid-scarred homes. They announced that they were ready to repeat this performance wherever such vandalism occurred in the city.

Interracial councils also help to create better attitudes. In Anderson, South Carolina, for example, a Council on Human Relations is set up on an interracial, interdenominational basis, and fifty to 165 attend the meetings. With a simple educational goal, the council helps Negroes and whites to communicate, says a leader, the Rev. Carl A. Pritchett, a Presbyterian.

Another practical technique used by church people in several communities involves signs. When panic selling of homes in the Germantown section of Philadelphia began, a Christian family called white and Negro neighbors together to form a council. They got signs, "This House Not for Sale. We Like It Here," and posted them in their windows. In Kansas City, Mo., a Presbyterian (U.S.), the Rev. E. T. Sturgess, printed similar signs: "Not For Sale! I believe in my community and neighbor!" He sold 150 of them to white families, at cost, and the exodus decreased.

¶*Church Schools and the Decision*

The race policies of church schools have recently had an especially strong spotlight on them, because of the Supreme Court decision and the recognition that these schools shape the future of the church. In general, the racial practices of church schools are somewhat better than those of church hospitals, which often exclude Negro doctors, nurses, and patients.

One of the most widely-publicized disputes involved the School of Theology of the University of the South, at Sewanee, Tennessee. In June, 1952, the university board voted forty-five to twelve against admitting Negro students. The Rev. F. Craighill Brown, dean, and seven seminary faculty members thereupon resigned. The Very Rev. James A. Pike, dean of the Cathedral of St. John the Divine in New York, also refused to visit the school to accept an honorary degree and speak.

For a year there was vigorous discussion. But in June, 1953, the vote was reversed; the board voted seventy-eight to six to admit Negroes. A Negro clergyman from South Carolina attended the graduate school that summer. The first to be admitted to the regular theological course was Merrick Collier of Savannah, described by Episcopal Bishop Middleton S. Barnwell of Georgia as "a fine young Negro, the son of a successful physician." The secular world took special note. The American Civil Liberties Union publicly cited the eight who resigned and Dr. Pike. The Episcopal Church now reports that all eleven of its seminaries, including three in the South, accept Negro students.

After Vanderbilt's School of Religion in Nashville and the Cumberland Presbyterian seminary were opened to Negroes, the National Council of Churches reported that at least ten Protestant seminaries in the South were admitting them.

Berea College, which was founded in Kentucky in 1855 by abolitionists around a fiery preacher, has long been integrated. Though nonsectarian, it is religious minded; the inscription on its seal is, "God hath made of one blood all nations of men." Even before the War Between the States, Berea was open to Negro students. Kentucky law prevented Negroes attending from 1904 to 1950, dates which remind us that school segregation has been a relatively recent phenomenon. But in its centennial year, Berea had sixteen Negro students.

The Washington, D. C., Friends School attended by the children of segregationist Senator James O. Eastland also announced that it would admit Negroes.

One means that churches have used to further school integration has been scholarship aid. The Evangelical and Reformed Church, for example, has a national youth project to assist young Negroes. In a recent year, Barbara Calhoun, a Cleveland music student, attended Heidelberg College in Tiffin, Ohio, where she served as guest organist in the churches; Jane Nabors, of Orange, New Jersey, was on the YWCA cabinet while attending Cedar Crest in Pennsylvania. This church reports that all six of its colleges, almost solidly white until recently, now have several Negro students.

The National Council of Churches has also helped considerably in recruiting students for a two-way integration project. This is sponsored by the National Scholarship Service and Fund for Negro Students. In the 1954-55 academic year, this organization helped enroll 110 Negro students in private colleges in the South, most of them newly interracial. At the same time, it aided eight white students attending Negro institutions. About six hundred white students are now enrolled in such schools.

In the South, the Universities of Maryland and West Virginia began admitting Negroes before World War II, and integration is now largely accomplished in higher education below the Mason-Dixon line. Professor Guy B. Johnson of the University of North Carolina reported that 125 Southern colleges, once all white, now admit Negroes. Almost half of these are church supported, and he estimated that close to a thousand Negroes attend the latter during the regular school year; many others attend summer sessions.

Leaders in several denominations have been pressing for a speed-up of integration since the Supreme Court decision.

Episcopal Bishop Angus Dun of Washington, D. C., announced a schedule for integration providing that applicants for Beauvoir School should be admitted into all grades regardless of race. In 1956-57 the policy is being applied in the beginning grades at two schools, and not later than September, 1958, all grades are to be opened.

After the court decision, the Northern Presbyterians' Board of National Missions reaffirmed its policy against segregation in its schools. The board reported mixed success in translating the policy into reality, however. It noted striking movement toward integration in three institutions in North Carolina, New Mexico, and Arizona, and a biracial student body is anticipated soon at Barber-Scotia College in North Carolina. Three Negro boarding schools in Georgia, Mississippi, and South Carolina are expected to drop segregation more slowly.

Oklahoma Baptist University was opened to Negro students in 1956. Some other Southern Baptist colleges and seminaries had integrated earlier.

In a survey, the *Christian Advocate* learned that fifty-seven predominantly white Methodist schools admit Negroes, but thirty-two do not. Seven schools that do are in Texas, Missouri, Delaware, Tennessee, Kentucky, and West Virginia.

"Negroes have been in our student body for two years and things have gone wonderfully well," said the president of Perkins School of Theology in Texas. "Other students and faculty are in hearty support of their presence."

Presidents of several segregated Southern schools told the *Advocate* that they may change, but slowly. The student body would now favor integration, some said, but older heads are opposed. "I believe we shall be making changes within six or eight years," one president reported.

Schools including Negro students were happy. A junior college in Vermont said that a Negro girl has received its highest award. An Alabama Negro boy was president of the student council at a New Hampshire school.

Action since the court decision has not been all for integration, however. Trustees of a Baptist college in North Carolina decided to continue to bar Negroes, and students at a Baptist university in Florida also voted against their admission. The Presbyterian Synod of South Carolina decided by a large majority to continue segregation "at this time" in two colleges and a seminary. On the other hand, the Synod of Florida voted to tear down race barriers in church membership and to urge trustees to consider admission of Negroes to its colleges.

A heartening illustration of how integration can come—and without prodding of the government—is the story of a Southern Baptist school in Texas.

Only white Anglo-Saxon students had been admitted to Wayland Baptist College in Plainview when J. W. Marshall became its president in 1946. Oriental and Latin American students began to come and met some objection in the community. When two cultivated young students from fine Mexican homes were refused service at a restaurant, the president tried to explain to them.

"I talked and talked and talked," he says, "but race hatred, discrimination, prejudice, segregation, all talked so much louder that I doubt that they heard a word I said. At times I couldn't even hear myself."

Sometimes a foreign student would inquire why there were no Negroes at Wayland. "Would a Negro student be welcome here?" the president asked the American students. They decided to have some informal polls to see, and results were encouraging. Then a Negro applied. The faculty was 100 per cent for admission. Of the students only eight were mildly opposed. But what about the trustees?

The president called the board members together and told them, "I know what our customs and traditions dictate, but surely to us there are stronger voices—the voice of democracy and the voice of Christianity." The trustees struggled with their prejudices, recalled the foreign students who had been in their homes, and voted to admit the Negro.

Now the question was: Would he be admitted, but segregated?

Wayland College decided to treat him as an equal. The

dining hall door was open to him. As other Negroes came, they were barred from local cafés and barber shops, but the two largest Baptist churches accepted them.

Parents welcomed them, too, and they were invited to the homes of white students. "Only two families, to my knowledge, have said, 'No,'" the president recalls. "The white sons and daughters in these homes were greatly humiliated. I am encouraged to believe that the majority of our parents are happy about nonsegregation."

What is the power behind this "miracle"?

"The greatest motivating force back of this bit of progress is the desire of Christians to be really Christian," says President Marshall. "When spiritual growth in America parallels our technical progress, walls of segregation will crumble to dust. I have seen a genuine religious faith quietly dissolve racial hatred."

8 A TYPICAL CITY—
CASE STUDY

L EN GORMAN, MANAGING EDITOR OF Syracuse's *Post-Standard,* called in a new reporter and gave him a curious assignment. He told him to go down through the Fifteenth Ward, then come back and tell him what he thought.

Fifteenth Ward refers loosely to the Lower East Side slum in Syracuse, a city of about a quarter million in the very center of New York state. It is one of those typical blighted areas of sagging houses and littered alleyways that lie at the heart of many Northern cities. Here live most of Syracuse's Negroes.

Walter Carroll, the reporter, had a striking background for the job. A thirty-one-year-old Southerner—he says a good Southern Baptist hymn still brings tears to his eyes—he had just arrived from North Carolina. There he had won a state press association prize for his feature story about the execution of a triple murderer. A one-time student of playwriting at Yale, he had worked on two plays with Negro casts in New York City, and was very much interested in the race question.

Carroll walked through the ward, saw the jerry-built tenements, noted especially the dingy café signs advertising Southern foods. Hundreds of the Negroes in the ward were newcomers to the North, migrant laborers who had come up to pick beans and had stayed on.

When he reported back to the office, Carroll was told to go to work on a series of articles. So he talked to slum dwellers whose children had died from rat bites. He looked at broken toilets covered with green bottle flies, counted six roaches on a child's pillow. He chatted, too, with people who felt that shiftless Negroes deserve such homes.

"My Southern accent helped," he recalls, "because men blurted things out before they knew where I stood."

Seven months he gathered material. An amateur artist, he drew stark cartoons to illustrate the series. Then on January 21, 1954, the first of his articles splashed on the front page under big headlines:

NEGROES' LACK OF HOUSING GIVES CITY
15TH WARD KEG OF DYNAMITE
Modern Ghetto Threat to Peace and
Progress—Race Riot Looms

The reverberations rippled out through the city. Day after day the blasts went on. Some Syracusans praised the stories, others deplored, but at least, all were awake. Carroll's vivid writing shook the apathetic and ignorant. Wasn't anybody trying to help?

Aside from the typical social agencies, one group, the East Side Coperative Council, was already working.

The Council, whose successes result from the efforts of a dozen dedicated persons, can perhaps best be portrayed by the stories of two leaders, one white, one Negro. Both are active churchmen, both are relative newcomers to the city. Progress here has been made not only by native Syracusans but especially by persons from Texas, Connecticut, Iowa, and other states; by Methodists, Presbyterians, Jews, Unitarians, Roman Catholics, and those of many other faiths. When people move around as they do now, no city is an island; the attitude of a man across the country from you today may be helping or harming you next door tomorrow.

Father Walter N. Welsh came to Syracuse in 1949 to be rector of Grace Episcopal, a white church in the Fifteenth Ward.

A Pennsylvania Dutchman, he grew up in a Reformed congregation in York but also sang in the boys' choir of an Episcopal church. When he was ordained in the Episcopal denomination, one of his great satisfactions was that a Negro rector was among those who participated in the service. For years he was in charge of youth work for the diocese of Newark, New Jersey.

What made him so concerned about the color bar?

"I am extremely interested in social justice," he says, "and this was where it focused. This was the area where I found I became really indignant."

When called to Syracuse, he was also named Episcopal chaplain at Syracuse University, just up the hill from the Negro ghetto and his church. He came with the "express purpose to relate the university and the community around it to the parish life." To do this, he immediately started getting acquainted with leaders of groups in the area. He joined an interracial cooperative—but that is getting a bit ahead of the story.

The year after the arrival of Father Welsh, Frank T. Wood Jr., arrived to become head of the Dunbar Center, an east-side community project. He is a well-dressed and well-educated Negro social worker. The lines of influence soon began to merge, for Father Welsh was interested in Dunbar, and he was among the first ministers Frank Wood met.

Mr. Wood found his way into social service by hard work and perseverance. The eldest of seven sons of a builder in Gloucester County, Virginia, he went through the eighth grade there, but because of school segregation, a Negro boy was unable to go higher. However, Frank went to live with an aunt in Norfolk and helped around her big boardinghouse to pay his own way through high school. Then he worked as a steward on a shipping line between Boston and Miami to meet his college expenses at Greensboro, North Carolina. After graduation in 1934, he went to the Atlanta School of Social Work, and sold underwear and insurance to support himself. He was director of a center in Poughkeepsie, New York, and later went to Syracuse.

At that time, police were troubled by a number of thefts, knifings, and other crimes in the Dunbar section. Mr. Wood checked with the chief of police to see what the center could do, then called together several ministers and representatives of organizations in the ward to talk over the problem. The idea of the East Side Cooperative Council was already germinating.

Meantime, Frank Wood was also making a church choice. He had grown up a Baptist (one brother is a Baptist minister), and he had taught Sunday school in Congregational and A.M.E. Zion churches. Some factors now drew him to Father Welsh's church. But deciding that he wanted to keep his roots in his own community, he joined a Negro Episcopal church in the ward. This was St. Philip's—a church that was, in fact, organized for Negroes years ago by the members of Grace Episcopal Church, and which now, ironically, poses a practical problem to Episcopalians like Father Welsh and Frank Wood who believe in integration.

Dunbar Center was started in 1920 by two sisters, members of a Unitarian church commemorating the Rev. Samuel J. May, an ardent abolitionist and friend of William Lloyd Garrison. Dr. May helped operate the old Syracuse station of the underground railway for escaping slaves.

One of those carrying on the Unitarian tradition of race relations today is Elizabeth Lewis, a sprightly, blue-eyed, white-haired teacher, not retired though nearly eighty. Born a Methodist and reared in a western New York home that was also an underground railway station, she came to study at Syracuse University in 1896 and soon joined May Memorial.

Miss Lewis was one of those who, in the thirties, started the Syracuse consumer cooperative that Father Welsh joined years later. This cooperative effort succeeded as one of the city's first organizations set up on an interracial basis. Another organization in which Miss Lewis has had a leading role is the Interracial Interchurch Fellowship, organized by church women to get white and Negro women better acquainted.

Father Welsh recalls that one of the first sparks in the chain reaction that led to the formation of the East Side Council was a meeting that this women's church fellowship called. It was held in the Christian (then "Colored") Methodist Episcopal Church, and the leaders were amazed at the crowd that arrived. Afterwards, the rector met the Rev. Eugene N. Goldstein, a Negro community leader, and they agreed that the unexpected zeal should be harnessed. A few months later, Gene Goldstein became the first president of the newly-organized East Side Council; later he was succeeded by Father Welsh.

Meantime, members of the Christian pacifist Fellowship of Reconciliation, especially Methodists and Quakers, called an interracial Family Life Conference at Father Welsh's church. From it grew a small interracial Family Group, whose members still meet monthly to discuss not race but the behavior problems that parents share, whether black or white.

¶Lines Converging and Crossing

Other lines from other cities and other denominations began to converge as the East Side Council was formally organized. From Philadelphia came an expert on race relations. He was the Rev. William H. McConaghy, who had been director of the Presbyterians' Institute on Racial and

Cultural Relations from 1948 to 1951 and now became pastor of Syracuse's First Presbyterian Church. A native of the Bronx, he attended Columbia University and Union Seminary. The first World Conference of Christian Youth in Amsterdam in 1939 gave him his real Christian conviction on the world-wide, integrated church.

Mr. McConaghy had hardly arrived in Syracuse before he was named chairman of the race relations work of the local Council of Churches. He soon became the churches' representative to the East Side Council and a member of the Dunbar board. He is also a member of the National Council's Department of Racial and Cultural Relations.

Mr. McConaghy has been called in as a church spokesman in half a dozen disputes about the movement of Negro families into white sections of Syracuse. In half of these, he says, the neighborhood integration has proceeded successfully.

"Syracuse is a typical Northern city in this matter," he points out. "Once the church people see the relation of principle and practice, they come around."

About the time Mr. McConaghy arrived, Mr. and Mrs. Donald Rumsey, who were to become virtually "Mr. and Mrs. Housing" in Syracuse, also came. Don, an engineer at the Carrier air-conditioning plant, was reared a Presbyterian in Winnetka, Illinois, and Barbara was an Episcopalian in Toledo, Ohio; they are now members of May Memorial. Something of their world concern is indicated by the fact that they have living with them, besides their own two children, a German law student and a ten-year-old Korean boy.

The couple had helped start an NAACP chapter in Schenectady, and before long Don Rumsey was chairman of the housing committee of Syracuse's new East Side Council. He and Gene Goldstein circulated a check list so that ward residents could see how their houses rated by legal standards.

"But the renters felt that they couldn't kick or they'd be evicted," Rumsey recalls. "The result was apathy."

Then came an incident that cut through some of the apathy.

In early 1953, Miss Mary Estes asked Miss Lewis if she knew anyone who might want to rent a small house on her property. Miss Lewis suggested that it be offered to a Negro family. Miss Estes, a Methodist who once ran a religious bookstore, agreed. Before long the family of a Negro welder, Roland Penney, rented it.

Then Miss Estes received an anonymous telephone call warning that the Negroes had better not move in or there would be trouble. She was frightened but stubborn. The Quaker meeting sent two people down to give her support. A small interracial gathering at Miss Lewis' house encouraged the welder to go ahead.

"Last night I was so bitter and so ready to tell people what I think of them," he told Miss Lewis after the meeting, "but now I feel good about them."

The threats proved hollow. The Penneys moved in and, for more than three years, they have proved good neighbors. The flowers around their little home grow attractively, and no one has caused them any trouble.

Someone meanwhile wrote the *Post-Standard* a letter calling slums the measure of social progress, on the theory that if people were not inferior, they would not stay in slums. Little did that writer realize what he was going to set off! Don Rumsey, incensed, drafted a letter in reply, and the East Side Council authorized him to send it to the paper. He proposed that the *Post-Standard* have a series of articles on housing. Later, he visited the leaders of the paper to press for the idea. Nothing came of it immediately. Reporter Carroll was just arriving in town.

However, another big idea was simmering.

After a meeting of the Dunbar board, one of the members, Benjamin Shove, stopped for a chat with Frank Wood. Mr. Shove, a native of the county, has taught Sunday school for decades in a suburban Baptist church. Socially prominent and attorney in a leading law firm, he is counsel for the New York State Council of Churches.

Lawyer Shove said he owned quite a bit of land in suburban Fairmount, next to the Community Church. He planned to give some to the church. Wouldn't it be a good idea to build an interracial housing project on the rest?

Frank Wood seized the idea. He knew a real estate man who wanted to help sell houses to Negroes. He found a builder, too. (Both were Roman Catholics.) Leaders of three banks were called in to a meeting at the Council of Churches. Shove was there, and so were Wood and McConaghy. And the bankers, tearing down a big barrier to Negro home ownership, gave assurance that they would provide mortgages for Negroes the same as for whites.

Then the Shove project ran into trouble. The people of Fairmount got wind of it. Many of them were newcomers to the city, with most of their savings invested in small homes. They didn't know nor care whether Benjamin Shove was from an old, respected family. Panic clutched them. Ringleaders got a sound truck out, and driving up and down the streets, they shouted that Shove was going to bring a flood of Negroes out into "$4,000 shacks."

The truth was that the houses would cost three times that, more than the homes of many of the protesters. And ironically, Frank Wood and Don Rumsey had been able to find *only four* Negro families with the money or interest to go into the proposed homes. There also happened to be some Negroes already in the Fairmount suburb.

But truth and reason were out. The protesters threatened to dynamite Shove's house. They made threatening calls to the Council of Churches and the Community Chest. Attorney Shove, harassed, decided to call it off.

The news of Fairmount went through Syracuse integrationists like an icy chill. Other citizens remained in blithe ignorance. The newspapers, perhaps because they felt it was too sizzling to touch, gave the development little or no attention. Probably nine out of ten Syracusans even today don't realize that the Fairmount incident happened. Still, the imbroglio doubtless bent the editors toward the idea of a series. The following winter, the *Post-Standard* dropped the Carroll blockbuster.

¶Community Profile

What kind of city did the newspaper series fall on?

Syracuse is a heterogeneous Eastern city. Surrounded by dairy farms, it has several large industries with a tradition of paternalism. Syracuse has an anti-union reputation, though the C.I.O. has made some progress. Politically, the city is a part of solid upstate Republicanism. Advertising men consider it a typical market and use Syracuse to pretest campaigns.

There are large blocks of Italians, Poles, Germans, Irish, most of them Roman Catholic. One priest, the Rev. Charles J. Brady, moderator of the Catholic Interracial Council, is especially active with Negroes. He has been outspoken in urging integrated housing, though some critics feel he has not gotten enough church support. However, Bishop Walter A. Foery of Syracuse personally paid tribute to Father Brady at a party honoring his interracial work.

Migrants have surged into Syracuse. Between 1940 and 1950, the Negro population more than doubled. Now six thousand or seven thousand, it is still only a little over 2 per cent of the total population of Greater Syracuse. Theoretically, this situation should not be a serious problem.

Most of the Negroes are jammed into the Lower East Side. Many whites live there also, but they can move out if they get the money and desire. The concentration in the ward is twenty-seven thousand persons per square mile, three times the density in the rest of the town. Businessmen are concerned that a 20 per cent section of the city's residential area accounts for:

> 60 per cent of all tuberculosis cases
> 55 per cent of juvenile delinquency
> 45 per cent of major crimes
> 35 per cent of fires

Like such areas of other cities, the ward provides only

6 per cent of real estate tax income; but it eats up 45 per cent of all city service costs.

If good housing is the Syracuse Negroes' chief problem, employment is doubtless second. Though fair employment laws have brought some improvement, Negroes tend to be held to unskilled employment. General Electric has some Negro engineers. Negro secretaries are now getting jobs. Since 1950, three Negro policemen and two Negro firemen have been hired, the first in town. Openings have improved enough for the East Side Council to have a ceremony honoring seventy-eight Negroes who received good jobs.

Because of the efforts of the State Commission Against Discrimination, the city's restaurants and hotels are now open to Negroes. Its newspapers avoid race labels, and sometimes even print Negro society photographs. Buses are unsegregated. So are schools. There are now four Negro teachers with mixed or all-white classes. However, high school fraternities and sororities are segregated by race and religion.

Many colored foreign students attend Methodist-related Syracuse University and live near the campus. All races participate in the chapel program; one chaplain, the Presbyterian representative, is a Japanese-American, the popular and smiling Rev. Arnold Nakajima (who lives in a "white" area).

This was the kind of city into which the Carroll articles plummeted. Neither especially good nor especially bad, Syracuse offers us a case study of how one typical community and its churches are reacting to the changing race picture.

Just a week after the newspaper series ended, fire raged

through an old East Side home cut up into crowded little apartments. A four-year-old child died in the flames. Over the whole front page, the *Post-Standard* editors painted this terrible proof of their warnings, with a dramatic three-column picture of a Negro minister comforting the bereaved mother.

In the late summer, Carroll took a job as a bean picker with a gang of migrants, and wrote another series. In September, he talked to a woman in one tenement who complained that she would be unable to get out if there was a fire; only a week later, she was one of two women who died as this very house burned! Bluntly, the paper went after the landlords of condemned dwellings.

Meanwhile, Republican Mayor Donald H. Mead had also taken action. Though business interests urging caution had considerable influence in his party, he ordered the building inspectors to work (after a five-year lapse in prosecutions for violations of building laws). Soon the city tore down forty substandard houses and another thirty dangerous East Side sheds. Fire calls in the ward dropped.

¶The Quakers Tire of Surveys

A significant move was also now starting in the Society of Friends. The clerk of the Quaker meeting was Adelaide Webster, who lives with her architect husband, Fred, in a streamlined house near Fairmount. Friends of Attorney Shove, they were appalled at the bigotry that had blocked his project near them.

Among others in the meeting who were eager to have the Friends do something on housing was Miss Lesley West, native Syracusan. Brusque in her speech and salty in her social criticism, she now asserted that she was sick and tired of the innumerable surveys of the East Side and wanted to see action.

The upshot was that the Quakers decided to call in an adviser from the American Friends Service Committee in Philadelphia. The possibility of a youth work camp in the ward was discussed, but the members soon agreed that the real problem was to help the Negroes move from the over-crowded ghetto into the white areas.

To do this, they hired boyish, sandy-haired Robert Hale, who was working for the New York Mayor's Committee on Unity. A native of Connecticut, he had attended Phillips Exeter and Harvard (class of 1948), with an interlude as second lieutenant in the Air Force.

Bob Hale came in the fall of 1954 and, supported by contributions of the Friends and friends of the Friends, he worked on Syracuse housing for six months. The Quakers appointed a committee to guide him and gave him a list of Negroes who were willing to move. He and a friendly Jewish real estate man telephoned persons with homes advertised for sale and asked them frankly whether they would sell to Negroes. Syracuse was surprised to learn that half the sellers said they would. Those who did object expressed fear of neighbor reaction; hardly anyone raised personal objections.

One thing Bob Hale soon found, however, was that it takes time to look, and Negroes are as particular as anyone when it comes to finding just the house they want. He dealt with a dozen families. He relocated only one.

Howard Smith, maintenance man at a tool company, liked a South Side house on Bob Hale's list. The owner was a woman moving to the Midwest and willing to sell. Smith and his wife took the house and spent time remodeling it before they went in. Everything has gone smoothly.

"One of the neighbors who peeked in through the window says it is the neatest kitchen in the neighborhood," Bob grins.

Though his score was only one, Relocator Hale had not failed. He had made the contacts and established a relocation system. Seeing the need to continue the work, Mayor Mead added him to the municipal staff when the Friends' money ran out. Hale became city director of relocation in March, 1955. Since then, he has helped literally hundreds to house-hunt. Many of them are from the substandard dwellings of the ward. About one fourth are Negroes. Each month twenty to fifty families on his list find homes.

Of course, not all of these have moved out of the East Side. Some have found other places in the ward. Bad as the area is, this is where friends are, and this is where many want to live.

"Migrants are like immigrants," Hale explains. "They don't want to venture out into the unknown away from their own kind."

He reported, however, that an increasing number of middle-class Negroes have different ideas: "Our office has been consulted by Negro physicians, Negro ministers, Negro engineers working at General Electric, a Negro professional basketball player, and a Negro college professor. I think it is safe to say that the desire or ability to move to other parts of the city exists only among this group, and a number have moved to various parts within the past few years. I can report, furthermore, that once in their neighborhood, these families have reported no neighborhood difficulty."

At the request of the Friends committee, a group of graduate students under Syracuse University Professor Kenneth Kindelsperger surveyed thirty Negroes who already lived in white areas. About a third had been in their houses from five to thirty years, but the survey showed that since 1951 or 1952, the movement out into the white sections had accelerated. Only two reported minor friction; twenty-eight said there had been no trouble. Some had integrated very well. One, for example, was president of the women's group at the neighborhood church.

Since Hale got the city job, only one case has threatened to explode. One tightly-knit neighborhood protested against a Negro buyer by expressing the usual fears of lowered property values, fears that have not been borne out in Syracuse or in other places where panic-selling is avoided. A brick was even hurled through the seller's window. But buyer and seller held firm, and as usually happens, the neighborhood found everything fine once the family moved in.

One relocated family, that of Fred Jones, a postal employee, bought a home in suburban Dewitt, which notoriously bars Jews from some sections. The way for the Jones family was smoothed by Mrs. John L. Ayer, a churchwoman who talked among her neighbors. When they moved, the Joneses were promptly received into the Dewitt Community Church, which already had one Negro family.

The total of Negroes scattered through white areas is now approaching fifty. Though this is about four times the number in 1950, the overflow from the ward helps little in relieving the pressure of the arriving hundreds.

The East Side Council looks to public housing as the only real solution for low-income families. But several sites suggested by the Mead administration have roused irrationally furious opposition.

Dissolving, the Friends committee organized a broadly-based Greater Syracuse Citizens Housing Committee to operate on a wider scale. The city has not yet solved its housing problem; but it has already demonstrated that a few dedicated people can pry obstacles loose if they really try.

¶Quiet Revolution in the Churches

While housing has held the headlines in Syracuse, integration has quietly been starting in the churches.

In 1950, there was apparently almost complete segregation in the Protestant churches of Syracuse. However, in the last few years—mostly, it happens, since the Supreme Court school decision—Negroes have joined or affiliated closely with at least a dozen churches of the community.

One of the oddest things about this movement to membership is that the community is virtually ignorant of it. Both Negro leaders and the ministers themselves are only beginning to realize what has quietly been happening.

Mr. McConaghy's church, First Presbyterian, might be expected to be in the forefront. But First, downtown on the West Side, is not near the Negro section, and he has not found it easy to make it an integrated church.

"We'll never settle the integration of schools and churches until we solve housing," he says. "The segregationists recognize it, and that's why they're so adamant in holding the line."

The first and only Negro in this church joined because her father, a Southern Negro Presbyterian minister, had asked Mr. McConaghy about her when the latter was on a visit to the South. When the pastor returned to Syracuse, he looked her up and found she was office manager of the YWCA. He invited her to come to the First Presbyterian Church. Margaret Cooper did attend about two years and sometimes brought Negro friends. Someone in the session finally asked why she didn't join and was told it was not because she hadn't been asked. Then at last, in 1955, she came into the church at the same time as a white YWCA leader.

"No one so much as commented," says the minister. "There just wasn't anything."

At the Rev. Arthur W. Mielke's church, fashionable Park Central Presbyterian, which is at the edge of the Negro section, a committee was appointed in 1951 to study the ward. Its chairman was Professor Floyd Carlson, one-time president of the interracial co-op. His committee suggested that a second assistant minister be named to work in the area.

When Professor Carlson became the church's representative on the East Side Council, the idea developed for the church to have a series of weekly dinner forums on the theme, "Who Is My Neighbor?" Speakers included the Rev. J. Oscar Lee of the National Council, William McConaghy, and Frank Wood. From 125 to two hundred, including Negroes from the neighborhood, attended these dinners. City-wide attention was focused on the discussions.

The Carlson committee suggested that a Negro be named assistant minister. But fears that the church would become Negro stirred the conservatives, and the session rejected the idea.

Hardly had this proposal been voted down, when a plant foreman, Bennett Teague, an unmarried Negro of middle years, decided to join. He was not urged by the ministers, but simply decided that this church was more to his liking than the Negro Baptist Church where he was a member. Negative reaction was insignificant.

Ahead of either of these churches, which had especially worked on the problem, was South Presbyterian. In the fall of 1954, a Chinese Presbyterian, Robert Moy, a General Electric engineer, and Mrs. Moy became members. About the same time, one of the city's Negro teachers, Ruth Bennett, began attending upon the invitation of several acquaintances. She joined the following February.

"She'll never force her way into any group," says the pastor, the Rev. Donald E. Wallace, "but if she's asked to help, she will gladly."

Because of her willingness, Miss Bennett sings in the choir, is program chairman of the senior young people's group, and teaches Sunday school. There has been a mild undertone of opposition among some elderly members, but most are enthusiastic.

"We've had young people say, 'She's just one of us. We don't even think of her color until someone mentions it,'"

Mr. Wallace says. "It's been a good education for our young people and the whole church."

A friend of Miss Bennett's, also a Negro teacher, Ann Brown, got a job in suburban Liverpool and teaches Sunday school in the Baptist Church there.

Frank Wood's wife, Peggy, a family worker for the Salvation Army, is the daughter of a Congregational minister and did not want to shift to the Negro Episcopal Church when her husband did. So she and the children accepted the invitation of the pastor of Danforth United, a Congregational-Disciples church.

There was no fanfare at all when the church accepted her, probably the first Negro to join a Syracuse white church. She is on the church youth program committee; and Frank Wood III, in his middle teens, recently served on the committee selecting a new minister.

After the Rev. Leon Adkins came to the University Methodist Church in 1950, its official board agreed to accept all who wanted membership, though it would not seek out Negroes especially. Before he left to become executive secretary of the denomination's Division of the Local Church, in Nashville, several Negroes had come into the church.

First Frederick Mayo, of the city tax bureau, and his wife, who had been reared in a white church in upstate New York, visited and decided they wanted to join; she became a Sunday school teacher and their two children attended. Later, Charles Ellerson, an eight-year-old, came to Sunday school and his grandmother joined him. When she attended a Bible class, others commented that she had "made the finest contribution in the group."

University Methodist has weekday released-time classes attended by many Negro children of its East Side neighborhood. One day a fourth grader among them said to Elizabeth Suiter, minister of education, "My mother wants to know if I can come Sunday." She was told she could, and the Sunday school was one bigger thereafter.

But Syracuse churches do have setbacks. An effort in University Methodist Church to start a Boy Scout troop for the interracial neighborhood failed after six weeks; infected somehow with prejudice, the few white boys stopped coming. Again, this and several other churches, including two Negro groups, held a vacation Bible school in an East Side park, and this time no Negro children came! Let no one think that all social barriers have dissolved.

Another Methodist church, far on the south side of the city, became integrated very naturally. The Rev. Charles R. Benton, pastor of St. Paul's, says that a Negro couple joined because housing segregation began to break down. Alonzo and Marjorie Carter moved into the white area of the church, without fanfare or trouble. They started attending St. Paul's, came for about a year, and in May, 1954, joined on confession of faith.

Near new public housing on the city's West Side, Centenary Methodist Church has also taken in three Negro members since early 1955. Ministers of the Council of Churches shared calls to these new homes, and the Rev. Lloyd V. Moffett found that one couple, Mr. and Mrs. William O. Divers, had been Methodists before coming to Syracuse. On his invitation, they attended and later joined. A mother whose children were attending released-time classes also joined. On Easter, 1956, downtown First Methodist accepted its first Negro member, though some Negroes had attended off and on for years.

The way housing and church attendance are linked is illustrated also by the story of Captain (now Major) James Walker of the air base near Syracuse. The Walkers, an educated Southern Negro couple, had to look a long time, but they finally found a suitable house in a northeastern section of the city, a mile from the ghetto. Because Eastwood Baptist Church was near, they began to attend there.

From time to time, Negroes from the base visit this church, says the pastor, the Rev. Nicholas Titus; once a Negro WAF sang in the choir for a while. But the Walkers and their children have attended for a longer period than any others. They have been well received at such affairs as Couples Club meetings, but so far they have not chosen to join.

A Negro girl has also been attending the Friends meeting but has not joined; a Korean engineer is the only nonwhite member of this society.

In two cases, whites are going to Negro churches. Two white families attend St. Philip's Episcopal, the church that Frank Wood chose. A white couple also joined the Christian Methodist Episcopal Church in 1954.

However, the Fifteenth Ward church of Father Welsh, who came with the intention of creating an inclusive congregation, is doubtless the most integrated of all those in Syracuse. It has been a struggle, however, and integration has not gone very far, even though Negroes live all around the neighborhood.

"I knew there wasn't going to be any rush, no matter how welcome we made them," he says. And he was right.

The rector even distributed flier invitations door to door "like an evangelist," but no one responded.

When Father Welsh arrived in 1949, the daughter and grandchildren of the janitor, George Hill, whose background is mixed Indian and Negro, were in the church. They were accepted naturally.

Then the family of Glenning Stokes, friends of the Hills, came; their small son, Eddie Stokes, became an acolyte. Next, members of two other families began coming. Dr. Charles Willie, a young sociologist at the university, who had helped the Friends housing group and who is the vice president of the East Side Council, came in. He and another Negro are in the choir.

But after more than seven years, Father Welsh says a little disconsolately, there are only five Negro members. A dozen or more Negro children attend this Sunday school regularly. The figures unquestionably give Grace Episcopal Church the record for integration in Syracuse.

But the net impression, whether considering housing or the church, is that the Negroes aren't going to "take over" anything in Syracuse, either the white dwelling areas or the white churches. Men and women of good will are going to have to keep pressing, in both white and Negro communities, to overcome the Northern brand of segregation and to create something a little closer to Christian brotherhood.

9 BUREAUS AND BROTHERHOOD

BLONDE, SIX-YEAR-OLD EVELINE HAD recently arrived from Europe. Now she was going off to Vermont with a group of New York City children who were being sent to the country by a church. Her mother was worried about how she would get along with new customs and children.

Eveline sat down in the train with Mary, a Negro girl about her size, who had a neat braid right over the top of her head. During five hours on the train they got acquainted. Toward the end, the little displaced person asked, "Please, may I stay in the same house with Mary?"

The adult with them did not know what had been worked out in town. But at the end of the

line, one of the hostesses called out: "I have two little girls—
Eveline and Mary—going with me. Where are they?"

The little girl with the white hair and the little girl with
the black hair jumped happily. And when the pastor went
round that evening to see how all the city children were
doing, Eveline and Mary were enjoying the country together, skipping and running on a big lawn, hand in hand.

Not a grandiose adventure, it was a typical warming
incident of the Baptist project known as Camp Friendly.
Under this plan each summer, more than one hundred children from the hot streets of New York, Boston, and Chicago
travel to Baptist homes in nearby areas. The children have
included American Negroes and whites, Arabs, Chinese,
and Puerto Ricans.

The Camp Friendly project is one of many activities
of the happily named Department of Christian Friendliness,
a ministry of the American Baptist Home Mission Societies.
In a typical recent year, 1,500 of its women volunteered to
call in homes of persons of a different color; a similar
number entertained students from abroad. Intergroup activities have been reported by 2,275 Baptist churches, and
363 nonwhite Baptists hold church offices, ranging from
deacon to caretaker, usher to education director.

In Chicago, reported Esther Davis, the department representative there, a concerned group in one changing area
decided to try neighborliness instead of "fright, fight, flight."
On the "block-group plan," all interested persons in a block
met to get acquainted and work together to improve the
community *for all*.

"Although the majority of our citizens now are nonwhite, we church people are saying, 'I like it here! I want to stay in Woodlawn,'" reports Miss Davis. ". . . I am experiencing a new sense of working together with new neighbors of different races, nationalities, and creeds, and it's wonderful!"

All the major Protestant bodies have similar work; we can touch upon only some of the highlights to illustrate some of the things being done.

The National Lutheran Council has a Division of American Missions that includes the Negro among its concerns. As indicated by the stories of Lutheran integration in Chapter 5, the division's position has been that the gospel should be taken to people where they are, and it counsels the Lutheran bodies about development of such mission work. In some cities Lutherans are forming Lutheran Interracial Service groups, to bring together those with a special concern for better human relations. They try to find interested, qualified persons to render Christian service in interracial or entirely Negro communities.

"A new day has dawned for the Lutheran Church in Negro and interracial communities," says a forty-page handbook. ". . . The thinking Negro is seeking more and more a church with an educational program and an orderly service."

In 1954, W. K. Fox, editor of the Disciples of Christ mission monthly, *The Christian Plea,* urged that Negro and white Disciples face the issues and do something besides pass resolutions. As a result, sixty-five leaders of four races in the first Disciples Conference on Desegregation came up with specific suggestions for agencies. Perhaps the major result was that these members gave serious attention not only to issues but to one another. One Negro pastor said:

"This is the first time I've ever really felt that white brotherhood leaders have listened or cared when I have something to say."

The denomination publishes considerable news of desegregation in its *Social Action News-Letter;* in one issue, for example, a Negro minister in Washington, D.C., the Rev. J. F. Whitfield, reported that one Disciples church there has received four Negro members, while his own church has a young white member. Mr. Whitfield's wife was elected president of the Ministers' Wives Group in the capital area.

The Evangelical and Reformed Church and the Congregational Christian Churches are in process of merging to form the United Church of Christ in the U.S.A. Early in 1956, before final approval of the union, they established through a Joint Committee on Race Relations policies to end segregation in the churches.

The Evangelical and Reformed Church in 1954 installed the Rev. Chester L. Marcus, a Negro pastor from Reading, Pennsylvania, as associate secretary for race relations.

The Congregationalists' American Missionary Association has a history of more than a century of work with Negroes, and in 1942 it established a Race Relations Department. This pioneered the race relations institute (the 13th annual meeting was at Fisk University in 1956).

The Congregationalists have also pioneered in cooperation with unions, government, and other organizations in overcoming segregation in society. For example, their researches furnished the findings and gave considerable impetus to the

order desegregating railroads. The denomination has issued
pamphlets on such controversies as interracial marriage and
integrated housing, and in 1955 the department mimeo-
graphed a lengthy memo for churchmen inquiring how to
make their congregations inclusive.

In 1952, the Presbyterians' Department of Social Education and Action published *Everyone Welcome,* a handbook
dealing with responsibilities for promoting Christian brotherhood. In 1955 a special 48-page issue of *Social Progress,*
referred to in Chapter 4, spelled out specific steps for desegregating. It summarized:

> Much has already been done and is being done by the General
> Assembly and in the boards and agencies of the church to bring
> about a nonsegregated church in a nonsegregated society. . . .
> Some presbyteries already have strategy committees which see
> and plan the church's extension program not only in terms of
> building new churches but also of conserving the old. . . . The
> church's missionary task should take its ministry wherever people
> live, including the inner city. The need for "new" churches (per-
> haps in old, abandoned buildings) which start out with a biracial
> staff of ministers and enfold, from their very inception, the hetero-
> geneous peoples at their doorsteps is not being met to any degree.
> Certainly here is one of the new missionary frontiers of our day.

In 1956 the United Presbyterian assembly urged congregations to offer full membership and fellowship to everyone
and called on church-related institutions to minister to "all
qualified persons." It also voted that appointment to staff
positions disregard racial lines.

In the Protestant Episcopal Church two subdivisions, the
Department of Christian Social Relations and the Division of
Christian Citizenship, cooperated to publish a booklet, *Just,*

Right, and Necessary, to interpret the Supreme Court decision to Episcopal congregations.

Of greatest importance [says the booklet] is an increasing, church-wide willingness to have an experience in nonsegregated activities. In many dioceses—South, North, West, and East—summer conferences are held on an integrated basis. All dioceses now include representatives of Negro parishes or missions in diocesan conventions.

Woman's Auxiliaries, young people's groups, and others are becoming more and more nonsegregated. The National Council employs clerical workers without regard to race and is the first American church body to appoint a Negro clergyman to a nonracial national post.

Peaceful community integration has been a special aim of the Quakers. The American Friends Service Committee has served especially in three areas—employment, education, and housing.

National attention has focused on one project in which Friends are helping. Over sixty-five persons, most of them Quakers, put up $150,000 to build 140 ranch houses on a fifty-acre plot in booming Bucks County, Pennsylvania.

Charles Henry, a machine operator, and his wife Victoria became the first Negro couple to buy in the county when they took one of these homes. Next door to them settled a white research engineer and his wife, George and Eunice Grier. The other homes are also being divided about half and half between majority and minority groups.

Said Quaker George Otto, head of the construction company: "I had a wonderful time giving Friends the opportunity of putting their money where their beliefs are."

The Church of the Brethren has recommended that people of all races be freely welcomed. Integration of Chinese, Negroes, and Puerto Ricans has begun at Chicago First Church, and Negro children belong to the Sunday school of Lower Miami Church in Ohio. A church with white and Latin leadership at Falfurrias, Texas, is now over half Mexican.

A Commission on Unitarian Intergroup Relations in 1954 reported fifty-two churches with Negro voting members, six of these in the South. Many had made a special effort to integrate. However, only twelve had five or more Negro members, and the commission declared "the need is greater than our accomplishments."

With interracial leadership, the Universalist Service Committee maintains in Chicago a community program for Negroes, Mexicans, Puerto Ricans, Jews, and Anglo-Saxons.

The Methodist Board of Social and Economic Relations deals with race questions, and its executive secretary, A. Dudley Ward, points out that the Council of Bishops, the general boards and agencies, and many churchwide gatherings are already interracial. Negro ministers participate actively as leaders in some conferences. The Woman's Division has successfully carried on interracial schools.

Yet there has remained for Methodism a unique internal problem. This springs from a compromise plan that brought Methodist union in 1939. White churches were organized into geographical jurisdictions, but Negro churches and annual conferences, already in existence, were put into a separate group, called the Central Jurisdiction.

In the fall of 1954, the Methodist bishops came out somewhat ambiguously for abolishing the Central Jurisdic-

tion and integrating the Negro churches. An Association of
Methodist Ministers and Laymen was formed in the South
to fight the move. For months debate boiled. Then another
arrangement was made. At Minneapolis in 1956, the General
Conference provided for an orderly abolition of the jurisdiction, provided the plan is ratified by enough annual conferences. It permits further breakdown of racial barriers by conferences and districts, where desired.

Already, some Methodists had taken advantage of a 1952
action of the General Conference providing for transfer of
churches from one jurisdiction into another more convenient
geographically. By such a transfer the Mitchell Memorial
Church, Negro congregation in Harrisburg, became a member of the Central Pennsylvania Conference. In New
York, eight Negro congregations, all in or near New York
City, were invited to join the New York East Conference.
This action was taken by white and Negro delegates of bodies
representing two thousand churches and almost half a million members. A Negro church in St. Paul was invited into
the Minnesota Conference.

The work of the various denominations is supported and
stimulated by a section of the National Council of Churches.
Supervising its Department of Racial and Cultural Relations
is a committee of about a hundred, representing various races
and denominations. The office is headed by an executive
director, the Rev. J. Oscar Lee, and two associates.

One of the department's chief functions is serving as a
clearinghouse. Each year the leaders respond to about two
thousand inquiries for information and advice from ministers, churches, teachers, and others. Through its retreat for

secretaries, it has aided in developing the strategy and program of the churches. The department also conducts three institutes each year that send laymen back inspired to improve race and cultural relations.

The department is perhaps best known for its sponsorship of Race Relations Sunday each February. The first such observance was on February 11, 1923, the Sunday before Lincoln's birthday. At the time, Negro and white Christians had little contact with each other, and the aim was to get them acquainted, to get them talking with each other. More recently the development has been toward making the Sunday a time when the churches plan year-round improvement in race relations.

Publication of literature is another big accomplishment. The department distributes nearly half a million pieces each year. It also issues a bimonthly *Interracial News Service,* a digest of trends and developments in human relations.

¶But Must We Love

Having seen how the churches struggle with the race problem in the many corners of their life, we come face to face with the ultimate question:

Is the Christian religion really opposed to walls of separation among the races?

The Bible does not provide easy, capsule answers. No verse says plainly and simply, "integrate" or "segregate." We have to interpret—and that's where the differences always begin!

Perhaps we can get some perspective by looking at what Christians say who have nothing to do with American race questions. Considering quite different problems, they infer that racial separation is a sin.

For example, the British Council of Churches has attacked segregation in South Africa as "against the Divine Law as set forth in the Bible." In South Africa itself, an Interracial Conference of Church Leaders made this statement: "We recognize and accept one another as brothers in Christ and avow our unity in Him." That is, "In Christ there is no East or West."

In this country, too, representatives of many different Protestant strains have called discrimination wrong. Presbyterians of Mississippi have declared "segregation is unchristian." The nation's largest Mennonite body attacked segregation as a sin directly contrary to Biblical teaching; prejudice, it said, "is a violation of the human personality as created by God." At Honolulu, representatives of the Protestant Episcopal Church resolved that segregation is "contrary to the mind of Christ and the will of God as plainly recorded in Holy Scripture."

The National Council of Churches, in a special message, has also warned that racial prejudice is not merely bad, unfortunate, or unrighteous, it is *sinful*. "Racial prejudice in any and all forms is contrary to the will and design of God. It is sin. Let this teaching be proclaimed. He who wrongs his brother sins against God."

But why does a Christian have to oppose discrimination? Can't Christians of different colors go their separate ways and still love God?

On these questions, the United Lutheran Church has made one of the most explicit statements of Christian principles from the conservative Protestant viewpoint, saying in part:

God the Father is the Creator of all mankind. We are made in his likeness. In the light of the common creation of all men, differences in physical characteristics or social background are only of incidental importance. . . .

God's atoning grace embraces every man. Through his Son, Jesus Christ, God offers redemption to all. Christ died for all mankind. . . .

Forgiveness through the cross restores men to fellowship with God. . . . The love of Jesus Christ, as revealed in the cross, leads men to the deepest kind of human fellowship and mutual service. . . .

God calls all men through the gospel to Christian brotherhood. . . . Love for one's fellowmen is the necessary counterpart of love for God. God calls men to serve him by serving one another.

In God's providence, Christians, different in racial, geographical, economic, and social backgrounds, may use their differences to contribute to the total enrichment of life. No group is self-sufficient. . . .

"That may be all right," someone objects, "when the kingdom of God has been established, but now—"

"We must live as if the kingdom already existed on earth as in heaven, or it can never come."

"Well, yes, but I'd still feel better if there were some out-and-out Bible verses that showed the way."

There is no real answer to that plea. There *are* the verses. But how we make them fit our preconceptions!

One of the strongest arguments against man's setting up barriers, for example, is Paul's reminder (in Acts 17:26, King James) that God "hath made of one blood all nations of men, for to dwell on all the face of the earth."

In that, the writer seemed to anticipate modern science (though the Revised Standard Version does not include the word "blood," the idea of the unity of man is the same). Science has known that the blood of all races is the same—the blood of a Negro may save a white, and vice versa. But even with science enforcing Biblical truth, one can hardly use this verse as proof; for it also says that God has determined "the bounds of their habitation." No doubt someone could make a case from that for the worst forms of segregation and even persecution!

No, you can't rest the case for brotherhood on a single verse. You have to look at the spirit of the New Testament. "The letter killeth," anyway.

As the editorial board of *Episcopal Church News* said in a unanimous declaration:

Those who attempt to justify segregation by Holy Scripture cannot avoid doing violence to the Bible as a whole. If they base their argument on the story of Noah's Ark ("They and every beast *after his kind* . . .") or that of the Tower of Babel ("The Lord scattered them . . .") or some other passage which seems to offer the segregationists support, the point of the whole books of Ruth and Jonah must be ignored. It then becomes especially important to ignore St. Paul's assertions about the unity of man in Christ. *There is neither Jew nor Greek, there is neither bond nor free, there is neither male nor female; for ye are all one in Christ Jesus* must be taken with something less than full seriousness by those who seek Biblical justification for segregation.

It is to this spirit of oneness, found in more than one verse, that the National Council of Churches refers in supporting its stand for a racially inclusive church. The brotherly attitude, it says in one statement, "finds its origin in the inclusive fellowship required by the Christian gospel, '. . . There can not be Greek and Jew, circumcised and uncircumcised, Barbarian, Scythian, slave, free man, but Christ is all, and in all.' "

A look at the attitude of early followers of Christ supports this view of the New Testament spirit. In the first place, the early Christian church seems to have been unbroken by race and class divisions. Paul preached in many countries to many different kinds of people; in Philemon, telling of the conversion of a slave, he appears to take a very brotherly attitude toward him. He writes the Ephesians that once they were "far off" but now "have been brought near in the blood of Christ." For "he is our peace, who has made us both one, and has broken down the dividing wall of hostility."

James, too, in the second chapter of his epistle, warns against undue "respect of persons" as a sin. The *Revised Standard Version* translates this as a warning, "Show no partiality." The point that James makes is against vaunting the rich, well-dressed man and snubbing the poor man. Can we be sure that, as he wrote, James did not have some tattered black slave in mind?

But behind the early Christians was Christ. Do we not find ourselves going back to Jesus himself if we try to grasp the spirit of the New Testament? What did he say and do about race?

Again, we find no red-letter verses directly on the race problem. But the fourth chapter of John tells how Jesus began to talk with a Samaritan woman at a well when his disciples went to buy meat. To her he was different.

"The Samaritan woman said to him, 'How is it that you, a Jew, ask a drink of me, a woman of Samaria?' For the Jews have no dealings with Samaritans."

Reminded of this segregation, Jesus might have desisted. But he didn't. He went on calmly speaking to her, so that when the disciples got back they "marveled that he talked with the woman." But she ended by saying that he was the Christ.

¶To Weasel or to Obey

"It may be necessary to speak to other races to convert them," one may protest, "but does it follow that we have to be friends with them? Does Jesus say anywhere that we have to be on a close, personal basis?"

"He says that first we must love God and then love our neighbor."

"And who is my neighbor?"

"A certain man went down from Jerusalem to Jericho, and fell among thieves, which stripped him of his raiment. . . ."

The answer, of course, is Jesus'. As Christ had not hesitated to talk to the Samaritan woman, now he did not draw back from making the hero of this parable also a member of this despised race. The priest and the Levite, the whites of their day, passed on the other side, but the man from the outcast group showed his love to God by loving his fellow man, and so inherited eternal life. Is it possible to read that parable in any way that will support living in separation from our fellows? Is not any such separation a passing by on the other side?

We may with interest speculate on the ethnic differences between Jews and Samaritans. Were the Samaritans perhaps darker? Or were they, living in the land to the north of Judaea, actually lighter, as people living in northern climates often are?

Certainly Jesus was not "white" in the Anglo-Saxon sense of the word today. In Palestine, I have seen immigrating Jews from remote Middle Eastern areas where they have not intermarried with Europeans, and they are a very dusky people. Perhaps, as foreign artists have visualized, Jesus too had a dark skin. But we see immediately that not knowing whether Jesus was lighter or darker than a Samaritan, or any of us, makes no difference to our faith. To the Christian, color can't make any difference.

Knowing that color doesn't matter, we can be sure that Jesus was not *excluding* those of *us* who are whiter when he prayed, "Our Father." The suggestion that he prayed only for darker peoples would be sacrilege. But neither did he pray for whites only. He prayed for all. As we are reminded by a dialogue that might take place between a woman and her conscience:

SEEKER: Our Father, who art—

QUESTIONER: Wait a minute, please! Do you mean just *your* father or our father?

SEEKER: Our Father, who art in heaven—

QUESTIONER: Do you mean Father of the Japanese, the Indian, the Negro, and the Russian?

SEEKER: . . . Hallowed be thy name, thy kingdom come—

QUESTIONER: Do you really want the kingdom to come

now? Will you personally pay the price? Are you prepared to be brother to all, to accept people on an equal basis? . . . .[1]

In the Lord's Prayer, we have the confidence that we are among the *our* of "our Father." But the same confidence requires that we exclude no one from our own *our*. That conclusion follows inevitably from the Christian idea of God. We are made, we say confidently, in God's image; something about us is like God. Does that mean that our whiteness is God-like? Or is it our blackness? Or our yellowness? Or is it not our humanness? Must God-likeness not be something to do with our souls rather than the color of our hair or eyes or skin? If any of us is in God's image, we would all seem bound to be. How can any of us draw lines of favor if God himself has not drawn them?

We not only say that man is made in God's image but that God is the Father of all. But if he is *our* Father, we must be brothers and sisters. The fatherhood of God necessitates the brotherhood of man. To rend the brotherhood is nothing less than blasphemy.

"We begin with the basic fact that we are children of God," Chester L. Marcus, the Evangelical and Reformed leader reminds us. "All Christians know that every man has inherent rights granted by God in creation. . . . From this creation we know that every man has intrinsic dignity and worth. Since this dignity and worth come not with the place or circumstances in which one is born, but from God who made him in his image, the violation of any man's person is tantamount to defacing the image of God."

It is this kernel of goodness in each of us, of God-like-

---

[1] From dialogue distributed by Baptist Department of Christian Friendliness.

ness, which unites us as men. "When Christ dies for someone," Harry Emerson Fosdick has said, "there must be something in him worth dying for." A look at the members of minority groups supports the faith in their real value as individuals. Men with black skins are no less intelligent than those with white, nor are those with brown or yellow. With equal opportunities, black and yellow and brown are no more disreputable or sinful or unclean than white. Science has demonstrated this equality, and American secular society is coming to recognize it. But even if a person is stupid and unclean and bad, does not the Christian have the duty to love him as a brother? Even if he is perhaps white?

By and large, American Christians will probably agree that we each have the duty to love. But must our charity really be personal, intimate? The inevitable question comes up: Won't it lead to intermarriage?

That question can be debated at length, but in the end is beside the point. We are not called upon, as Christians, to plot how good actions will result, any more than a doctor must consider whether a patient will live a sinless life before healing him. We are not required to second-guess God. Leave it to others to be cunning and prudent. We are to be as little children, to take "no thought for the morrow." We must have faith that obedience to God's will leads, not to evil, but to good. We are commanded to love our neighbor, and what will come of our acting in love toward our neighbor must be left to God.

Would missionaries ever have gone out to foreign lands, one wonders, if they had worried about whether their children might grow up and marry native converts? Did the Good

Samaritan stop to ponder whether his daughter would marry the man who had fallen among thieves?

Simply to ask such questions shows that the speculation about the future of the races cannot be advanced as a serious argument against acting in Christian love. Love must come first. When fears of racial mixing are advanced, they already threaten to become idols, to replace God's place as *the* Eternal. And God is not mocked. Those of us who are white—a minority in the world—may well tremble when we reflect upon the workings of the just wrath of God because we have knelt before the calf of whiteness.

When we turn to the God of Mercy for guidance, we inevitably come to the Golden Rule. Without worrying about the cost, we are told to do unto others as we would be done unto—no exceptions for color mentioned.

Of course, we often *do* worry about the cost of being Christian. We sometimes try to rationalize away our guilt about segregation by telling ourselves that perhaps Negroes want it. Those of us who are white would not like others to force us into separate schools or trains or churches but, we ask ourselves, if we were Negroes, wouldn't we prefer "our kind"?

Surely the essential meaning of the rule cannot be bent to uphold separation. Have we who were born white, and who have taken the church from its dusky founders as our church, a right to maintain it exclusively as if it were only ours? If we had been born black, would we feel it right for others to draw a circle around their church and shut us out? If Christ was dark, would those of us who are white feel it Christian of colored peoples to exclude us from his sanctuaries? Would we not feel that Christ bound them to seek us out, regardless of our pinkish color? To ask the questions is to answer them.

Finally, we must seek the spirit embodied in the Sermon on the Mount itself. Jesus was not, like Moses, a lawgiver. He came not to destroy the law but to fill it out. He gave us a spirit greater even than the rule of treating others as ourselves. Men had been told not to commit adultery, but he said not to look with lust. Men had been told not to murder, but he told us to love our enemies. We were to turn the other cheek, to go the second mile. Always we were commanded to do more than the obvious or the least.

We are to seek the spirit of the beyond, the most. We are to give the cloak also. When we are confronted with the demand to treat the Negro or the Indian or the Chinese as an equal, we may not begrudge equality. We are to give more than asked. We are to put ourselves last. We are to be friendly; more, we must treat people of different colors as brothers under the Father. We are to love. In love for God, we are to go out and actively seek and struggle to find ways to show loving-kindness for all men, no matter how humble.

This is the great command upon us.

ABOUT THE FORMAT

The text of this book is set in Caledonia, a face designed by the distinguished American graphic artist, W. A. Dwiggins. Although it is similar to Scotch Modern in some respects, it is a distinctly modern face, freely drawn and clean cut in character.

Composed, printed, and bound by BOOK CRAFTSMEN ASSOCIATES, INC., *New York. Jackets and paper covers designed by* JOSEPH ESCOURIDO *and printed by* AFFILIATED LITHOGRAPHERS, INC., *New York. Text paper,* S. D. WARREN'S OLDE STYLE LAID. *Typographic design by* MARGERY W. SMITH. *Binding by* LOUISE E. JEFFERSON.